MASTER
OF
CAPE HORN

Upon a morning once in May,
Glancing up for'ard,
I saw a clipper in the bay
Nor'west-by-nor'ard.

No sound she made, that dawning
   bird;
No engine ranting;
Her song was sung without a word,
Silently canting.

The beauty of her bow alone
Carving each white horse
Like whetted razor on a hone,
Called back the old Norse.

We have no vessel now to match
That tall-rigged glory,
Nor any yarn of any watch
Capping her story.

J. H. B. Peel, *Bird of Dawning*.

Homeward bound. Signalling for a pilot off Falmouth, 1901. Painted by Captain James Nelson, O.B.E., of the Blue Funnel Line, who served an apprenticeship in square-rig under his famous father Captain William Andrew Nelson.

MASTER OF CAPE HORN

The Story of a
Square-rigger Captain
and his World

**William Andrew Nelson
1839–1929**

by

HUGH FALKUS

LONDON
VICTOR GOLLANCZ LTD
1982

To the Nelson family

British Library Cataloguing in Publication Data
Falkus, Hugh
Master of Cape Horn: W. A. Nelson 1839–1929.
1. Nelson, W. A.   2. Seamen—Great Britain—Biography
I. Title
387.2'2'0924   VK140.N/

ISBN 0-575-03089-5

Photoset in Great Britain by
Rowland Phototypesetting Ltd, Bury St Edmunds, Suffolk
Designed by Graham Brown
Colour plates printed by
White Quill Press, Mitcham, Surrey
Black and white plates printed by
BAS Printers Ltd, Over Wallup, Hampshire
Text printed by St Edmundsbury Press
Bury St Edmunds, Suffolk

CONTENTS

COLOUR PLATES

Frontispiece

Signalling for a pilot off Falmouth, 1901. Painting by Captain James Nelson.

Following page 14

Brig *Jessey* of Whitehaven approaching Malta in 1848, painted by A. Cammillieri.

The full-rigged ship *Annandale*, painted by William Huggins.

James Jardine, painted by James Nelson.

Following page 80

Auchencairn, painted by Godfrey.

Mary Moore in 1888, by an unknown artist.

Acamas, painted by James Nelson.

Paddle-tug *Florence* towing the barque *Grimello* into Maryport during the gale of 18th October, 1883. Painting by William Mitchell of Maryport.

Following page 96

Ladas, painted by James Nelson.

Barque *Inverness* off Beachy Head, painted by James Nelson.

BLACK AND WHITE PLATES

Following page 48

The *Southerfield* on the stocks in Messrs Ritsons' yard, 1881.

Launching of the *Point Clear*.

Maryport waterfront c.1890.

Maryport in Victorian days.

Three topsail schooners in tow outward bound from Maryport, c.1890.

The salvage of the damaged four-masted barque *Hougomont*.

Hougomont safely berthed in Maryport harbour.

The *Auchencairn* under full sail.

The *Auchencairn* at anchor.

The first *Oceanic*.

Auxiliary schooner *Henry Scholefield*.

William Andrew Nelson, c.1875.

Captain Nelson and his wife, Jane, c.1881.

Captain John 'Seadog' Jackson of Whitehaven.

Captain Robert Dixon, photographed in San Francisco about 1880.

Seaman John Leece, aged 95.

Following page 112

The *Mary Moore* at Melbourne, 1934.

The harbour at Iquique, about 1880.

The *Brier Holme*.

Vallejo and Broadway wharves, San Francisco harbour, towards the end of the nineteenth century.

Captain John Rich.

The *Hougomont* at Maryport, c.1903.

The harbour at Portland, Oregon.

Acamas on the stocks in Messrs Ritsons' yard in 1897.

The crew of the *Acamas*, San Francisco, 1903.

Captain and Mrs W. A. Nelson at Queenstown, 1905.

Fitting out one of the new Maryport steel-built 'working ships'.

The barque *Ladas* when under the ownership of Rasmus F. Olsen.

William Andrew Nelson, retired but undiminished.

Ninety, but still the same undaunted look.

Twin-paddle steamer *Manxman* leaving Maryport harbour.

Acknowledgements

For help with the preparation of this book I am deeply grateful to Miss Annie Robinson M.B.E., J.P., popular Maryport historian, who provided several rare photographs and documents as well as much local information; also, to Mr Tom Leece, former Maryport sailor and lifeboatman, for his memories of Captain William Nelson.

For information about the Nelson family, I owe a special debt to Miss C. I. Dixon, granddaughter of William Nelson, and her mother, Mrs M. Dixon, the Captain's only surviving daughter. For other family information and for the ship paintings by Captain James Nelson, O.B.E., my warmest thanks are due to William Nelson's other granddaughters, Mrs J. Ceha, Miss M. Nelson and Mrs K. Sampson.

I am indebted to Miss Jane Jackson for details of her great grandfather, Captain John 'Sea Dog' Jackson, and to his great grandson, Mr Charles Donovan, for the splendid painting of the brig *Jessey* of Whitehaven. The picture of the *Henry Scholefield* was kindly provided by Mr R. F. Jackson. For the picture of Captain J. H. Rich of the *Brier Holme*, together with accounts of his voyages, I must thank his great grandson, Mr K. H. Rich. For the plan of the *Mary Moore* and historical photographs of Iquique and San Francisco, I am indebted to Mr David R. MacGregor. Photographs of the harbour at Portland, Oregon, are reproduced by kind permission of the Oregon Historical Society. I am grateful to Captain Harold D. Huycke of Edmonds, Washington, U.S.A., for assistance in tracing these old photographs.

I am most grateful to Mr R. S. Oldacre and to Mr Arthur Oglesby for their photography; to Dr Sheila Nelson Marsham and Dr Rodney Gallacher for help in matters medical, and to William Nelson's great grandsons, Phillip Nelson Marsham and James Nelson Marsham, for help in matters mathematical.

To the Department of Trade and Industry Examiners of Masters and Mates, for information on the examination syllabus, I must express my gratitude; also to the staff of the National Maritime Museum, in particular to Mr A. W. H. Pearsall, who traced Captain Nelson's logbooks and discovered details of his ships. I must thank, too, Miss D. Hazlehurst of the Archives Department of Ocean Trading and Transport Ltd, who so happily supplied information on Blue Funnel matters, together with some missing pages of Captain Nelson's memoirs.

For their kind help, I am greatly obliged to Miss Corinne Miller, former curator of the Allerdale Museums; Mr Frank J. Carruthers of Cumbrian Newspapers, and the Cumbria County Council Archives Department.

I am grateful to Mr J. H. B. Peel for permission to quote his poem 'Bird of Dawning'.

Finally, I must acknowledge the invaluable help of Captain Nelson's grandson, Dr Thomas Nelson Marsham, C.B.E., to whom credit for this book is mainly due, and whose patience and kindness passeth all understanding.

Cragg Cottage
1982

Bibliography

A History of Seamanship, Douglas Phillips-Burt.
The Last of the Windjammers, Basil Lubbock.
Clipper Ships, David R. MacGregor.
Sails and Sailmaking, Robert Kipping.
Maritime Maryport, Annie Robinson, M.B.E., J.P.
Maryport Harbour, Lieut. Commander B. G. Ashmore, R.D., M.A., J.P.
A History of Maryport, Herbert and Mary Jackson.
A Dictionary of Sea Terms, A. Ansted.
The Solway Firth, Brian Blake.
History of Whitehaven, Daniel Hay.
Seafaring Under Sail, Basil Greenhill and Denis Stonham.
Blue Funnel, Francis E. Hyde.
Ocean Passages for the World, Rear-Admiral Boyle T. Somerville C.M.G.
British 19th Century Marine Painting, Denys Brook-Hart.
No Gallant Ship, Michael Bouquet.
The Oxford Companion to Ships and the Sea, Peter Kemp.
Nicholls's Seamanship.
Know your own Ship, Thomas Walton.
The Ship: The Life and Death of the Merchant Sailing Ship, Basil Greenhill.
Notes upon Losses at Sea, Francis Elgar.

FOREWORD

by Dr Thomas Nelson Marsham, CBE

'If this is what happens to you ashore, then I am going back to sea,' said my grandfather, Captain William Andrew Nelson, having just retired at the age of sixty-eight, on catching what he claimed to be his first cold. And back to sea he went to complete forty-seven years in square-rigged sailing ships, thirty-six of them in command.

It was typical of him. A determined man and a seaman first and last. About my grandfather's own life and attitudes there is little I can add to his own memoirs he partly scribbled down in old log books and partly dictated to his daughters at home or when they were aboard his ships on the coastal legs of his voyages, particularly as they have been so skilfully interpreted and put into context by Hugh Falkus in this book. There is, however, one additional aspect I would like to mention, having heard and experienced something of it at first hand: his ability to inspire others and to pass on his own high standards of seamanship.

As a boy in Maryport I met some of the old seamen who had sailed with him. On the harbour piers, in the intervals between attending to the infrequent demands of our cod-fishing lines, they would pass the time recalling their lives in sailing ships and his voyages. There were tales of the way he led them to make fast passages of which they were extremely proud; but, more important, tales of more desperate occasions when they freely acknowledged that their survival had depended mainly on his ability to inspire flagging crews to accomplish feats of endurance and seamanship they had not believed possible.

I know, too, of the impact he made on his own son, James Nelson, and on his future son-in-law Thomas Brabban Marsham (my father). These two fine seamen, who remained life-long friends after being apprentices under my grandfather in his ships, the *Acamas* and the *Ladas*, thereafter shared similar careers, serving in the Royal Naval Reserve and becoming masters at the same

time in that fine Liverpool shipping line Alfred Holt and Company. Although
these two men were professional seamen, not romantics, I think a genuine
love of ships and the sea assisted them in their profession—a love which to me
shows so clearly in James Nelson's beautiful ship paintings. These pictures,
often painted on the backs of old charts, were done simply for his own
pleasure and appear outside his family circle for the first time in this book.

I heard both my father and my uncle James speak many times of the debt
they owed to Captain Nelson for the training he gave them. Indeed throughout their own distinguished careers, during peacetime and two world wars,
they demonstrated to the full their inheritance of what Hugh Falkus calls the
supreme professionalism—that exceptional ability and seamanship which for
consistently successful voyages is required as much in power-driven vessels
as in sail. It is largely as a tribute to these men as representatives of the finest
aspects of our merchant seafaring tradition, to which we all owe so much, that
this book has been produced.

PREFACE

The Solway Firth, that stretch of treacherous sandbanks and tidal currents linking north-west England with south-west Scotland, is flanked by numerous small ports, today mostly disused, but a hundred years ago flourishing in the hey-day of a busy maritime trade. These inlets and harbours included the Isle of Whithorn, Kirkcudbright, Kippford, Dumfries and Annan on the Scottish side, with Silloth, Maryport, Workington, Harrington and Whitehaven on the English side.

While sailing in this part of the Irish Sea, which is now almost devoid of shipping, I have often thought about the great days during Queen Victoria's reign when the sailing vessels and crews of the Solway ports were famous throughout the world. Their numbers were astonishing. Indeed, I do not think that any other local stretch of British coast can have produced so many fine ships and sailors as those of the Solway shoreline.

Of the harbours themselves, it was Maryport first and foremost that seized my imagination. This tiny town of hilly streets and narrow lanes, birthplace of Thomas Ismay, founder of the famous White Star Line—home port of Fearon, Dixon, Rich, Messenger, Tweedie, Collins, Hardy, Briscoe, Sewell and a host of other great sailing-ship captains—once supported no fewer than four ship-building yards, whose tall vessels included some of the finest windjammers ever built.

But of Maryport's illustrious list of seamen, one in particular attracted my attention: Captain William Andrew Nelson (1839–1929) whose commands included some of Maryport's best-known ships.

My interest in this magnificent seaman began simply because much of my Solway sailing was done aboard the yacht of one of his grandsons, Dr Thomas Nelson Marsham, whose father Thomas Brabban Marsham—himself a master mariner who, as a boy, served as apprentice in two of William Nelson's ships—had married Jane Nelson, one of William's daughters.

Through Nelson Marsham's kindness I was able to study what remained of Captain William Nelson's seafaring records and log books, which had been preserved by William's son, Captain James Nelson, and discovered in James's papers after his death in 1957.

Before going to sea, James Nelson, who, like his friend and future brother-in-law Thomas Brabban Marsham, had been an apprentice under William Nelson, had served his time as a draughtsman in Messrs Ritsons' Maryport shipyard. He was a gifted artist, and the beautiful paintings he made of his father's ships (as well as some of his own) illustrate this book. Later, James served as second mate in the barque *Inverness*, and later still—like his brother-in-law—became a master of great distinction, commanding ships of Alfred Holt's Blue Funnel Line and finishing at the end of the last war as Holt's Chief Nautical Adviser. It is thanks to him that we have his father's memoirs and abstract logs.

The more I studied these records the more astonishing they seemed. Until the Panama Canal was opened in August, 1914, the route to the Pacific lay round Cape Horn. The speed of William Nelson's windjammer passages, beating westwards on this fearsome journey to the nitrate ports of South America, combined with the high degree of safety both of ships and men, appeared almost incredible. As I compared the accounts of his voyages with those of many contemporary ship's masters, and as my knowledge and understanding of this indomitable little Cumbrian sea captain increased, I became convinced that here was a most exceptional man. Furthermore, that in his professional record, so closely bound up with Maryport and the Solway coast, there was a fascinating story.

To appreciate the magnitude of his achievements we must take into account the maritime background of his age. Britain's seaways in Victorian times were vastly different from today's.

Looking out across a sweep of empty sea from William Nelson's old home on the Maryport Brows, it is hard to credit the number of sail that would have been in sight a century ago. Full-rigged ships, barques, barquentines from the Solway ports, bound to and from the Americas, Australia, the Far East; and mixed with them, engaged in coastal and continental trade, a fleet of brigs, brigantines, topsail-schooners, ketches and smacks.

In Maryport now, the once bustling docks lie rotting and deserted. Yet here in William Nelson's time great ships were being built and rigged; their sails stitched in local lofts, their iron-work fashioned from locally smelted metal. They were local men who built and owned the ships and local men who

Brig *Jessey* of Whitehaven (later commanded by Captain John Jackson)
approaching Malta in 1848, by A. Cammillieri.

The full-rigged ship *Annandale* 338 tons. Built 1826–7. Painting by William Huggins (1781–1845).

James Jardine painted by James Nelson.

crewed them, and their fame spread round the world.

What Maryport did was not unique. In nearby Workington and Whitehaven and in so many other towns and villages around the coast of Britain, something similar was happening. And what was achieved by local British shipwrights and seamen of that bygone age is part of this story.

The shipping lanes of the windjammers and early steamships were the arteries through which the life-blood of these islands flowed. In conditions of the greatest hardship and danger, the men who sailed those ships took Britain's commerce to the ends of the earth.

It is right that they should be remembered.

Maryport

I

A spirited little Town

Maryport, the Cumbrian Solway town that became William Nelson's home for most of his long life, was typical of the small, bustling, overcrowded but rapidly growing British seaports of the 19th century. Named in 1756 after Mary Fleming, wife of Humphrey Senhouse, Lord of the Manor, Maryport had been managed by members of the Senhouse family since its humble beginnings as a coasting haven exporting coal in the early 18th century. In 1833, however, an Act of Parliament placed the management and control of both the town and the developing harbour under a Board of Trustees.

Together with representatives of the Senhouse family, who owned the land Maryport was built on, this 'District and Harbour Board' was comprised of members elected by the town's ratepayers and shipowners. A secret ballot introduced for the Board's election gives Maryport a claim to the first official use of such a voting system.

In his newspaper the *Maryport Advertiser* of February 18th, 1870, Robert Adair who, with a companion, had been responsible for instigating the secret ballot of 1833, wrote in an editorial:

> Forty years ago we had, in connection with another, a great struggle to establish the principle of vote by ballot at our Trustee elections. So satisfactorily has it worked in Maryport, up to the present time, that no one would think of substituting the system of open voting, and our mode has been since adopted in many other towns and in Australia. This week, Mr Leatham's Ballot Bill was introduced in the House of Commons and was read a first time.

Two years later, the Act of 1872 made a secret vote for public elections compulsory throughout the country.

During the latter part of the 18th century and the early 1800s Maryport's trade steadily increased. This was mostly in coal, brought to the coast from neighbouring mines by donkeys and pack horses. The population was small and Maryport in those days was considered a very healthy place. According to an article in the local paper dated May 19th, 1865,

> Many persons have attained to a very great age living here. In the year 1790 one was living to the age of 112 and another 107. About the same date there was a flourishing cotton manufactory employing between 400 and 500 people; besides, some years earlier, Maryport could boast of a large pottery, glass works, salt works, and iron smelting furnaces . . . In 1747 there were only 64 families settled in the whole parish. But in less than 50 years after that period there were 685 families, and above 3,000 inhabitants; and about 90 vessels belonged to the port, averaging 120 tons burden. Their chief trade was the carrying of coals to Ireland; but they also shipped iron and glass to distant ports.

In 1836, to accommodate the ever-growing number of ships, a tidal dock was built with a swing-bridge across the entrance. It had an area of just over two acres.

Ships were first registered at Maryport in 1838, and on February 3rd, 1842, this little huddle of houses on the estuary slopes of the River Ellen finally shook off its association with neighbouring Whitehaven—to which, previously, it had been a subsidiary port. From now on, over the next fifty years, Maryport prospered and grew in importance; iron ore, timber and grain forming most of its imports; its exports being mainly iron rails, general cargoes and coal.

In 1843 an Admiralty survey was carried out and some improvements made. By 1853 the number of ships arriving at the port had increased dramatically and the need for better facilities became urgent. A new dock (the 'Elizabeth'), the first floating dock in the country, was opened on October 20th, 1857.

Some idea of how many sailing vessels were using Maryport and other Cumbrian harbours soon after this can be gathered from a report in *The Maryport Chronicle* of February 15th, 1861:

> The gale which commenced on Friday night last has not been equalled for fury and intensity within the memory of the oldest seaman . . . For the previous two or three weeks we had a succession of heavy winds from the south and south-west, which prevented vessels leaving the Cumberland ports; the consequence was that the harbours of Maryport, Whitehaven and Workington were crowded with coal-laden vessels. To such an extent was our harbour blocked, that coal-shipping had for some days been entirely suspended. When the wind was observed to change on Friday, an unusually large fleet of vessels put to sea, upwards of 80 left Maryport, and we are informed that 140 left Whitehaven . . .

And only three years later, the *Maryport Advertiser* reported:

> There have been upwards of two hundred sail of vessels in Maryport harbour at one time during the last week, and many of very large tonnage. These vessels, be it known, have not been driven hither by stress of weather as to a harbour of refuge, but they are all here for the legitimate objects of trade. The dock is crammed, and the old harbour, even above the bridge, is crowded with vessels; yet owing to the want of room all trade is at a standstill—there being no possibility of moving the vessels to and from the loading berths.
>
> We last week inserted an article from a correspondent on the subject of harbour extension, and we have since been informed that the article has the entire approval of the maritime community; and the prevailing wish is to have a new dock on the north side. This is a growing opinion, and should not be any longer disregarded by the trustees.

In 1874, when the harbour revenue had reached over £6,000 and was increasing annually, a report on the proposed new 'north side' harbour was made, but the project came to nothing. Eventually, it was decided to build a new dock on the south side, and on February 26th, 1880, Mrs Elizabeth Senhouse cut the first sod.

In 1884 when this new dock (the 'Senhouse') was opened, the tonnage of imports and exports was 378,807 with a revenue of £9,952. Six years later the tonnage totalled 1,038,754 and the revenue £34,503.

Much of this prosperity derived from the town's export of coal from local mines, and ironwork from local foundries. But it was the ships it built that made this tiny town world-famous. Shipbuilding was Maryport's chief industry—for which it had become self-supporting; all necessary rigging, ironwork, ropes and sails being made locally.

The first Maryport shipbuilder had been William Wood who in 1765 launched the brig *Sally*, of 106 tons. Wood's was the only shipyard in Maryport until about 1780, when he was followed by John Peat. Peat flourished until 1840, and to him must go the credit of achieving the earliest broadside ship-launch. This unusual and exciting method of launching, which attracted huge crowds, was later to give the town an unparalleled reputation in maritime circles when, among many other fine ships, such big four-masted barques as the *Peter Iredale* (1,994 tons) and Captain William Nelson's famous *Auchencairn* (1,925 tons), were successfully toppled over sideways into the narrow channel of the River Ellen.

That John Peat was the first shipbuilder to use this method is confirmed by a report in *The Cumberland Pacquet* of 25th October, 1803.

On the 3rd instant, a fine new ship was launched from the building yard of Messrs Fletcher, Fawcett, Peat & Co at Maryport (called the 'Anthorn' for Capt. Scaife), which for the rumour of its novelty and the uncommon fineness of the weather, attracted an amazing concourse of people, a greater number it is supposed than has ever been seen at that place since it became a town. The launching was not in the usual manner, the vessel descended broadside foremost into the water from a perpendicular height of between three and four feet, and afforded a very curious as well as pleasing sight to the numerous spectators.

Joseph Middleton, whose daughter Charlotte married Henry Ismay, grandfather of Thomas Henry Ismay, founder of the White Star Line, opened a shipbuilding yard in 1810. He built many vessels, but seems to have done little work after 1828.

Messrs Ritsons, the pre-eminent firm of Maryport shipbuilders, was started by John Ritson in 1830. In 1840 he was joined by his sons Robert and William. William Ritson was said to have been able to demonstrate to any workman how every shipbuilding tool should be used, from a caulker's mallet to an adze.

In the *Maryport Advertiser* of October 6th, 1854, Robert Adair describes in rich Victorian prose the midnight broadside launching from Messrs Ritsons' yard of the full-rigged ship *John Currey* (1,000 tons) on September 9th—an occasion undoubtedly attended by the young William Nelson.

Every workman of the establishment was at his post at 12 at night. The novelty of a night launch attracted large numbers who thronged the surrounding embankments . . . The two senior partners silently paced the deck of the ship, filled with hopes and fears of the issue, while the junior (William Ritson) hurried with torch in hand and encouraged this man and rallied the other, amid the incessant rattling of a hundred hammers. When the rattling ceased at one o'clock a solemn silence reigned and, with the last dread stroke, and fall of the spurs, the boldest held his breath for a time.

The huge mass began to creep on her cradle, slowly, as if reluctant; the ways too were creaking under the ponderous weight and a breathless silence pervaded the multitude in the grandeur of the quiet moonlight. On the ship's first kissing her destined bridegroom Neptune, on this her nuptial night, one universal burst of applause rang from the heights to the ship and again re-echoed from the occupants of Moat Hill. As the vessel increased her speed down the ways, and the massive chain was dragged after her the links in collision sparkled like a train of gunpowder, while the bursting wedges were flying in all directions . . . She adds another laurel to the chaplet of fame long since won by the justly celebrated firm which built her.

Alas, in October of the following year (1855), the *John Currey* became a total wreck in the Malacca Strait.

John Ritson died in 1844 and William Ritson in 1866, but Robert Ritson carried on successfully, later taking his sons John and Thomas into partnership. After his death in 1887, the firm continued to prosper under John and Thomas, and it was from 1885 onwards that most of its largest and most famous vessels were built. The last Ritson vessel, the steel steamship *Lycidas*, was launched in 1902.

Following the Ritsons, William Walker took the yard over and launched eleven steamships. The last two vessels built in Maryport were the steamships *Rhenass* and *Silverburn*. The *Rhenass*, in April 1914, was the town's final broadside launching. The *Silverburn* was launched, endwise, on August 8th, four days after the declaration of war on Germany.

That very briefly is the history of Maryport's shipyards and the shipbuilders who so greatly increased the town's reputation and prosperity. But if, as an influence in maritime affairs, mid-Victorian Maryport had surged forward, it had at the same time, in its own domestic affairs, remained lamentably backward. According to the memoirs of Frederick Kelly (1851–1930), for many years Maryport's Town Clerk and, later, Clerk and Manager of the Harbour Commissioners, Maryport was the last Cumbrian town of any size to provide itself with a satisfactory water supply and sewerage system.

Little more than a hundred years ago the town's general living conditions and sanitation were appalling, with frequent outbreaks of cholera and typhoid fever. Both these diseases commonly spring from sewage contaminated water. Situated on the sides of steep slopes, Maryport was naturally placed for an infected water supply, and the chances of disease—already heightened by inadequate sewage disposal—were increased, as in any seaport, by the steady influx of ships from overseas. As with the neighbouring ports of Workington and Whitehaven, the 19th-century increase in trade, while improving Maryport's material prosperity, helped to maintain a horrifying death-rate, especially among the local children.

This was the world in which the young William Nelson found himself when the family moved from Annan at the end of his schooldays in 1853. What he made of it is not on record, but certainly he seems to have come through his boyhood unscathed by the diphtheria, TB, cholera and enteric fevers that carried off so many of his contemporaries.

Little is known about William's education, but he is said to have been very good at mathematics—which goes some way towards explaining the never-failing accuracy of his celestial navigation and the ease with which he passed his Board of Trade examinations.

We know that after leaving school—the Annan Academy—at the age of fourteen, he worked from 1853 to 1860 as an apprentice sailmaker in the Ritsons' sail-lofts. We know, too, that the Nelson family, like most of the shipmasters and their families, lived at the top of the town close to the cliff 'brows' overlooking the sea. Life was undoubtedly safer up there. There is no doubt, either, about William's scrupulous attention to personal hygiene. According to his surviving daughter, Margaret, he was a great believer in cleanliness and bathed every day, even at sea—most unusual behaviour for someone of that time.

Despite a life expectancy that for many progressed no further than early childhood, Maryport's population in sympathy with that of other British towns during the Industrial Revolution had constantly increased. When William Nelson came to live in it the town had a population of between five and six thousand, and was entering the period that led to peak prosperity.

There was no shortage of work, although wages and living standards were meagre. A carpenter, providing his own tools, was considered well paid at 24/- a week. Labourers earned from 14/- to 16/- a week. Farm labour was cheaper still. The workmen were mostly employed in the shipyards or as coalminers, sailors, railwaymen. Prices in 1860 reflected the current value of money: per pound, beef and pork were 6d; potatoes ½d; butter 1/-; plaice 2d; cod 3d; flour 2/- a stone; turkeys 3/- each; Gin was 11/- a gallon; whisky and rum 13/-; brandy 27/-. Over fifty years later, food prices were almost identical.

Like prices, hours and wages were fixed; modifications difficult to obtain. In 1853, when Maryport's shipyard workers struck to have their weekly wage of 22/- increased to 24/-, the rate being paid to the shipbuilders of nearby Workington and Whitehaven, their 'industrial action' caused a considerable stir. And when, much later, the carpenters forced their employers to give them a half-day off on Saturdays, it so peeved the shipyard owners that the bell signalling 'cease work' was not rung— although the men stopped just the same.

As indicated by 700 signatures objecting to a new water-scheme in 1867, Maryport people tended to stick together. However misguided the objection may have been, 700 from a total population of about 6,500 represented a high proportion of the rate-paying males. (The women of those days—with the exception, it seems, of Mrs Senhouse—had little say in matters of public importance. Whatever influence they may have had was in private, on their 'men of affairs' husbands, and kept very much in the background.)

Whatever they were up to, the people of Maryport were strongly partisan, and their civic pride was reflected in their work. The town was justifiably proud of the ships it built, and the men who sailed them. Without question, Maryport produced not only some very fine ships but some very fine sailors.

In his *Notes*, hand-written in beautiful copperplate script at the end of the last century, William Russell (1827–1907) says of Maryport:

Never in its history could the town boast of possessing much wealth, but we can boast of its enterprising men who have risen to positions of independence and influence in the world, many of them born of poor, but honest hard-working parents.

Later, Russell reflects on the Maryport he grew up in:

Maryport in the year 1832, the year that has always been known as the year of the first cholera, which carried away a great number of inhabitants, was a small town numbering from three to four thousand. Travelling shows, Mountebanks and Caravans used to perform on the Green, which was also a playground for the young. The enclosing of the green for a burial ground would be about the year 1835.

A direct result, doubtless, of the first 'awful visitation' of cholera.

I remember when the Old Court House was opened for trials. What a great number of people used to watch the policeman bringing the poor fellows from the lock-up to the place of trial. Our lock-up was built into the side of the Brow—[a hill near the harbour] a sad damp place to put any human being into. The York City and District Bank stands on a site in the centre of the town where there was a large yard where pigs were kept. No wonder there was a bad smell in the bank, being built on such a dirty place . . . Nearby a very dirty property was the site of some small houses one storey high. The people who lived in them made their living by bringing coals with donkeys from the colliery in the District, the donkeys living under the same roofs . . . Other dirty places used to be the stabling for the Globe Inn; the loft above the stabling was where the Travelling Play Actors used to perform . . .

Maryport was lighted with gas before our wealthier neighbouring town Workington, but our Harbour used to be called by the Workington and Whitehaven seamen a Gutter, on account of it being so narrow. The first Dock we had built is what is now used as the Elizabeth Dock Basin . . . The first vessel that entered it was built and launched in Wood's Ship Building Yard. She was brig rigged, having been masted on the yard, with flags flying from trucks to deck, and a Band of Music on board playing. All her yards were manned, the guns firing, the music playing, the people hurrying as the gallant vessel entered the Dock. This was a red letter day for the town and Harbour of Maryport.

In that passage we glimpse the England of yesterday, when people took a fierce pride in their work—and were not ashamed of it.

We had a good coal, timber and cattle trade to this port. It was an amusing sight to see them discharging cattle from the vessels . . . Each vessel had a waist-board which could be removed when required. They removed the cattle from the vessel's hold by a winch and a rope strop round their bodies, laid them on deck, removed the strop and rolled them off the vessel's deck into the water. When they arose to the surface they had a look about them and then swam to the bank, the Bullock Men being there to look after them. I have seen as many as four vessels discharging cattle at one time . . . The spring of the year used to be a very busy time, when the vessels were fitting out and every trade was busy. There was no sending out of the town for goods. Everyone was anxious to spend their money in the town, and let their own townspeople have the full benefit. Would that it was more so today . . . There used to be four shipbuilding yards employing a large number of men and boys . . . The vessels built here were considered second to none for strength and desirability. Mr T. H. Ismay's father was foreman of Mr Middleton's yard. He married Miss Sealby when he commenced business as a shipbroker. He was the first shipbroker in Maryport. Soon after that he became a ship owner.

The first railway we had in West Cumberland was the Maryport and Carlisle. I distinctly remember the day when the first three sods were cut. There was a Procession of gentlemen and workmen, the latter carrying spades over their shoulders, accompanied by a Band of Music . . . There were several barrels of ale on the ground. The thirsty ones would not allow time to have them tapped in the ordinary way, they put some of them on end and broke the ends in and bailed it out in anything convenient. It was a rough time with the drunken men going about the streets . . .

The first vessels that took on board the first coals brought by rail were the *Fly* of Harrington and the *Betsy* of Maryport. The *Betsy* was my father's vessel. Each vessel was flying a flag with the name of the Colliery.

This end of the line was worked long before the line was through to Carlisle, on account of the coal traffic, about 1840. Before the railway was opened, coals were shipped by carts. Our quay used to represent a very busy appearance, with such a number of horses and carts being engaged in this trade. The coal carts had to come through the town and go the same way back. As each cart was emptied into the vessel the cartman received a Token from the Mate, and got paid at the Colliery Office according to the number of Tokens he had.

Many of our vessels in the Timber Trade used to carry passengers to North America from Cork, Sligo and Belfast . . . An occasional vessel carried passengers from Maryport. At this date there were no large Atlantic Liners sailing; neither from the

Mersey nor the Clyde, as there are today. What a change. Instead of having a 40 days passage or upwards, it can be made in under 6 days now.

I could have mentioned many other improvements and have contrasted Maryport's present condition with what it was before the outbreak of cholera in the year 1832, when so many of the inhabitants died. Today the town is sewered. We have a plentiful supply of good water, leaving no excuse for having either dirty houses or dirty clothes, or even dirty persons . . .

We have a Promenade second to none in the County. If you are wishful, any clear evening you can see the prettiest sunset that can be seen in any part of this England of ours. We have now Docks that are the envy of the neighbouring ports, who a few years ago spoke of our Harbour being a gutter. We can now berth vessels in our Dock carrying from 4,000 to 6,000 tons of cargo. I knew the Harbour when a little vessel of 68 tons burden could not leave the port during neap tides for want of water.

I should say that the town possesses more wealth now than ever it possessed at any time in its history. And now in conclusion let me say to all young people: never let the enterprising spirit of your forefathers die out. Retain that spirit amongst you and try and retain the proud name the town has born in the past. The spirited little Town on the Solway.

It was this 'spirited little Town' with its harbour, its slipways and its ships, that for seventy-six of his ninety years was the home of William Andrew Nelson.

2

The Solway Nelsons

William Nelson's connections with Maryport and the Solway Firth sprang naturally from a family that had been associated with these waters for many centuries. The Nelson ancestry was Norse. From a Fergus of Galloway whose father was Somerled (a Viking name meaning 'Summer Voyager') they became the Neils of Galloway, the name becoming Neilson and eventually Nelson during the 16th century, when the family still lived on the Scottish shore of the Solway.

For upwards of 300 years the Nelsons maintained a continuous seafaring and mercantile tradition, extending their interests from the Scottish to the Cumbrian side of the Solway and later, in the 19th century, to the growing port of Liverpool.

William's grandfather, Philip Nelson, built the Salterness lighthouse, the oldest in Galloway, which marked the last dangerous headland on the approaches to Annan. This lighthouse is now called 'Southerness'—less appropriately, for the corruption loses the connection with the salt-making that once took place there.

The family of William's father—Ben Nelson, who was a shipping merchant as well as manager of an Annan bank—were involved in the construction of what became the Carlisle Canal, which linked the city with the Solway Firth at Fishers Cross. Originally, it was intended to do this at Maryport as part of a grand scheme to link that thriving Cumbrian port with Newcastle—a project never fulfilled. That such a canal, with no less than 117 locks running across the Tyne gap, was ever considered, was probably more of a tribute to the growing importance of Maryport than to their knowledge of the civil engineering problems involved.

The Napoleonic wars affected the Nelson family in a variety of ways. One Nelson had the misfortune to be captured by the French while running supplies into Gibraltar. Other members of the family were more fortunate, being engaged in some brisk trading with Europe by breaking the French blockade. These profitable ventures were paralysed by the advent of peace.

The setback was only temporary. By 1823 the Nelson fortunes were on the rise again in the shape of the brigantine *Britannia* sailing out of Annan. Soon after this they built the *Annandale*. She is described in a letter written sixty years later by Dr Philip Nelson to his nephew Jonathan (also a sea captain) from Solway Cottage near Annan on 21st May, 1888.

> In 1826 my father laid down a vessel of 338 tons register called the *Annandale*. She was built in a potato field at Annan Well—was ship-rigged and fitted out for the East India trade. She was launched at the beginning of August, 1827 and sailed in December for Bombay . . . I possess an oil painting of her by the painter to King William the fourth, Huggins by name, and I have directed it on my death to be handed over to you.*

During Victorian times there was nothing unusual about building a ship in a potato field. In those days, small vessels were being built in fields as well as on creeksides and slipways and beaches all round the British coast. By far the greater part of the world's commerce was carried by small vessels of 500 tons and under. Like the *Annandale* these ships were for the most part neither built nor manned in the great seaports, they belonged to much smaller ports and havens. As often as not they loaded and discharged their cargoes on open beaches. Michael Bouquet describes them in his splendidly evocative book *No Gallant Ship*:

> They were financed by local capitalists, built by local craftsmen and commanded and manned by local mariners. They were as integral a part of rural England in many counties as the village churches, the markets and the mills, the farm wagons or the

---

*As a young man, Huggins was a seaman in the service of the East India Co. and made many drawings of ships in the Far East. Later he set up as a professional painter, being expressly employed to make drawings of ships in the East India Company's service.

He was a prolific painter, using strong, glowing colours on white canvas and paying careful attention to detail. Marine painter to King George IV and to William IV—for whom he painted large pictures of the Battle of Trafalgar—he exhibited at the Royal Academy in 1817 and continued to exhibit occasionally until his death.

A pleasing story is told concerning Huggins's draughtsmanship. Turner, who had been commissioned by King George IV to paint Trafalgar, produced a canvas of great dramatic and poetic grandeur but rather less marine accuracy. After the king had presented this work to the Greenwich Hospital (now the National Maritime Museum) John Ruskin declared it to be 'worth all the rest of the Hospital, building and pictures together.' His naval pensioner guide, however, was not so impressed. 'It's all right, sir', he said simply. 'But we really ought to 'ave 'ad an 'uggins.' (As seamen, the Nelson family would never have left themselves open to that riposte!)

village smithies. They ranged from small coasting smacks, carrying about fifty tons of cargo on short local trips, to ketches and schooners for coasting and the near Continental trades, to brigs, brigantines and barquentines for deepwater, and to small barques of 400 to 600 tons, capable of sailing to Australia or around the Horn . . . Their story is one of an origin in the local, rustic shipowning of eighteenth-century England; of growth in the forties and fifties of the nineteenth century; of a splendid flowering in the sixties and seventies, and thereafter of a slow and gradual decline in the face of changing economic conditions and new methods of transport.

No records of the *Annandale*'s trading have survived, but she must have proved a profitable venture. For the Nelsons to have commissioned her portrait from William Huggins, the famous marine painter to both George IV and William IV, implies success well above the average. (A fine painting it is, too. Happily, still in the family's possession.)

With such a seafaring background it was natural for William Andrew Nelson and his younger brother Benjamin to fancy a life at sea. From the earliest age, it seems, both boys knew what they wanted to do. Even his father's insistence on his being apprenticed for seven years as a sailmaker when he left school at the age of fourteen, did nothing to discourage William. Indeed, as he had the foresight to realize, this training in ropes and canvas was to prove an invaluable asset when it came to driving ships hard in heavy weather.

A few years later, Benjamin, too, left school and expressed aspirations similar to his brother's. Sensing, perhaps, that he was faced with the inevitable, Nelson senior placed no obstacles in the way of his younger boy and Benjamin went straight off to sea as an apprentice.

In 1853, the Nelson family had moved to Maryport. This suited the careers of both boys. While William was serving his time in Ritsons' sail-lofts Benjamin served his time in the *Hazard*, a Maryport vessel which belonged to a local man, Captain Johnston Melmore, and was engaged in the coasting and Baltic trades. He rose quickly and on gaining his master's certificate, sailed for many years in the Quebec, Montreal and West Indian trades, commanding vessels for both Ritsons and a Mr John Abbott of Penrith. He also had a vessel of his own, the *Atlas*, which sailed in the Quebec timber trade.

Benjamin certainly had his share of adventures. On one occasion while in command of the barque *John Abbott*—the ship was called after its owner—in the face of great danger he rescued the crew of a Norwegian barque, the *Hafrsfjord*.

The incident is described in a newspaper obituary of 1913:

Captain Nelson's ship was on the passage home from Quebec when he observed a vessel in distress. Getting to windward of her he found the vessel on the point of sinking. There was 18 feet of water in the hold, and all the boats had been smashed in an attempt to launch. A heavy gale was blowing, and the night was dark and thick, but Captain Nelson was not going to leave the ship's crew without an effort. A volunteer crew manned the *John Abbott*'s lifeboat which was launched after great difficulty.

It was impossible to get near the sinking ship in the sea that was running, but the Norwegians—including the Captain's wife—jumped into the sea, and were hauled into the boat by ropes. Two journeys were necessary, and all were saved but one man who was carried away before he could be caught. Before morning came the Norwegian barque had sunk. The 18 rescued persons were landed at Troon, at which place Captain Nelson was presented on behalf of King Oscar of Norway and Sweden, with a beautiful silver-mounted telescope as an appreciation of his services.

Another occasion on which Benjamin was instrumental in saving many lives was not long after his appointment as Harbour Master at Maryport. A barque, the *Estrella de Chile*, had left Whitehaven for the River Plate with a cargo of steel rails on Sunday, 24th November, 1888. Watching her progress, Benjamin noticed that the wind was backing southerly and that the ship, making leeway in the rising storm, was in danger of being carried up the Solway towards shoal water.

Sure enough, at first light the following morning in very thick weather, Benjamin glimpsed the *Estrella*, as he thought, aground on Robin Rigg bank. He immediately summoned the lifeboat crew; but, by the time they had assembled, the ship was hidden from view by driving rain and cloud. No signals of distress had been seen or heard, nor had the ship been spotted by anyone else. In consequence, there was some hesitation in sending out the lifeboat on what many thought to be a fruitless journey.

What followed is typical of the Nelson spirit. Confident that the ship he had seen was the *Estrella*, and in a situation of great danger, Benjamin boarded the tug *Senhouse*, saying: 'We must do the best we can. If you will follow, I will lead the way.' Whereupon the lifeboat was launched and taken in tow. A press account takes up the story:

> Under Captain Nelson's guidance the wreck was found, and not a moment too soon. The crew of the doomed ship were in the rigging and had given up hope, but all except one were saved.

The dead man was the mate. He had lost consciousness and fallen from the mizzen rigging three hours before the lifeboat's arrival.

A newspaper article of the time cites another of Benjamin's adventures. This time with icebergs in the North Atlantic.

> His vessel was bound for Halifax with a cargo of salt when she struck an iceberg head on. The vessel's bowsprit was splintered three times, and as she passed along the great berg, her yard ends were scraping the ice. It was a most thrilling incident. Huge masses of ice overhung the decks, threatening every moment to crash down and send the vessel to the bottom, but by skilful work the ship was got clear, and reached Halifax safely. Captain Nelson was a successful shipmaster. To native courage and ability he added a thorough knowledge of his craft, and a genuine consideration for every member of his crew. Ashore he was equally esteemed and respected.

There is no doubt that Benjamin was an accomplished, considerate and gallant ship's captain. But notable though his career was, it was overshadowed by that of his brother, William.

To understand how this came about, to appreciate fully quite how great a windjammer captain William Nelson became, it is necessary to grasp something of what seamen in those days were up against, of what life at sea in 19th-century merchant ships was really like. And this demands a chapter to itself.

3

The lonely sea and the sky

William Andrew Nelson's seafaring career, from 1862 to 1909, spanned the last great days of sail—from the clipper ships of the sixties and seventies until the domination of steam propulsion at the beginning of the 20th century. It was an age whose like will never be seen again. An age of dramatic contrast.

We speak of the 'great' days of sail. And indeed great they were. Great was the performance and great the appearance. A sailing ship was an artefact of breathtaking beauty; perhaps the most aesthetically satisfying commercial vehicle man has ever made. It was also, probably, the most dangerous; certainly the most uncomfortable. Although appealing in her loveliness, the distant beauty of a ship at sea hid the ugliness of life on board.

At this stretch of time, it is difficult to imagine quite how dreadful the conditions of service could be for a windjammer's crew in 'the good old days' a hundred years ago. There are few ways-of-living today that can be compared to the sheer hell of life in an average 'limejuicer' fighting her way to windward through a Cape Horn winter.

For the miserable, half-starved crew, ill-clothed, ill-housed, feet frost-bitten as likely as not, fingers raw from clawing at iron-hard, flogging canvas, there was no respite from the relentless pounding of wind and water. Soaking wet day after day, night after night, lacking any form of comfort, their beds nothing but bare bunks, with, perhaps, only a 'donkey's breakfast' for a mattress, they struggled simply to survive; while the ship, staggered along under lower topsails and storm jibs, the wind howling in her rigging like a devil's lament above the constant roar of the sea.

It was horribly easy to go overboard, to be lost at sea. A man could lose his grip aloft or miss his footing. A wave sweeping the deck could take several men at a time.

Most vulnerable of all were the apprentices. Many came straight on board a sailing ship with no previous experience, often from families with no seafaring tradition. Some, perhaps, were carried away by the romantic aspects of popular adventure stories; stories that suddenly lost their glamour on a topgallant yard in the icy darkness of a Cape Horn gale. A misjudgement, a slip, a rotten gasket, a rope torn from numbed fingers . . . death came all too easily to boys unprepared for the harshness of a big windjammer. And it came all too often. Not counting those lost in missing ships, thirty-six apprentices died in 1905. Thirty-six in one year!

There was another side to it of course. There could be (as John Masefield wrote) 'a grey mist on the sea's face and a grey dawn breaking.' And stun'sail days of trade winds and blue skies and flying-fish, when they ran their Easting down.

But the sun on the back of a windjammer seaman did nothing to improve his conditions of service: to put food in his belly, or increase the pitifully meagre wages he pocketed, if he pocketed anything at all, when 'the long trick' was over. (Yes, Masefield himself served in square rig. But only the one voyage. That was enough for him. He never went back.)

He was lucky. He found he could write. Most deck-hands were not so lucky. For many of them, gaol was the only alternative. And some of them may have preferred it. After all, a prison—even a Victorian prison—could hardly have been worse than the conditions in some of the ships they sailed. At least it was *safe*! Even so, however hard the life and even though the shore was for ever beckoning, time after time most of them (albeit with the 'aid' of the crimps) found their way back to sea.

Once the sea had bitten them the love/hate relationship with their ships could be real enough. Living and working conditions before the mast were harsh in the extreme. Nevertheless, there really was romance—of a sort. The sea could breed meanness and avarice and brutality, but it commanded respect. In many men it brought out the worst. But in some it brought out the best, and the best could be very fine indeed.

Not all seamen were hopeless sots; not all mates, bucko bully-boys; not all masters avaricious skinflints with ill-timed chronometers, out-of-date charts and a reluctance to work up star sights! There were seamen, sailmakers, carpenters who were proud of the work they did and the ships they sailed in. There were honest masters of compassion and immense ability, who cared for their crews and treated them with humanity. Such a man was William Nelson, arguably the most outstanding windjammer master of all time.

To achieve such distinction in one of the toughest jobs on earth demanded exceptional qualities. Determination, knowledge, seamanship, guts— William had these in plenty. A natural aptitude, too, for he came from a centuries-old Solway family with a great seafaring tradition. But there was something else. 'Genius' is an overworked word. Better, perhaps, to call it supreme professionalism. Like his naval namesake of an earlier age, William Nelson had an extraordinary flair—not only within himself but in his ability to inspire others, to instil in them something of his own very special quality.

In the comparatively sturdy, unspectacular ships he commanded—more fully-lined vessels than the famous tea clippers of the sixties and seventies— most of them built in a tiny Maryport shipyard and launched beam-on into the narrow River Ellen, Nelson made passages that challenged not only those of larger and potentially faster sailing ships, but many contemporary steamers.

Among these Maryport vessels was one of the earliest four-masted barques, the *Auchencairn*. Commanded by William Nelson during the six years she worked under the red ensign, she did some great sailing. Once, outward bound to Australia, she averaged ten knots for twenty-five days on end. Three times in two years Nelson sailed her between Britain and Puget Sound, and once to San Francisco, in less than four months—when other ships were taking five, six and even seven months.

In his book *The War with Cape Horn*, the late Alan Villiers—himself a master in sail and an authority on mercantile history—wrote:

> None of these ships that W. A. Nelson sailed so well was a 'clipper' (the *Mary Moore* came nearest to that but she was a carrier too, or Maryport would not have bought her). They were working ships, long-haul cargo-droghers of coal and grain, lumber, nitrate, cement, railway iron: and the good passages were part of their economy. The *Auchencairn* never did a better day's run than barely over three hundred miles, yet she ran 7,100 in thirty-one days on a two-and-a-half month passage to Australia. She made San Francisco sixty-one days from Port Pirie, far up Spencer's Gulf in South Australia. She consistently moved big cargoes through the great seas at economical speeds on worthwhile voyages, and the grace with which she did these things appealed to master and ship's company. He was a *satisfying* master to serve with, *all* his ships were satisfying ships ... A lucky fool might make one good passage, but only an outstanding shipmaster showed consistency.

There is no doubting Nelson's log books. According to Captain Nelson's grandson, Dr T. N. Marsham, Alan Villiers (who probably studied more sailing ships' logs than any man alive) commented: 'Masters tended to exaggerate their daily runs. But the logs of William Nelson are never in doubt. The distances he claimed to have made good, he made.'

Apart from accurate navigation and an eye for weather, there was only one way a master could make such consistently fast passages—by keeping as much sail set as possible until forced to shorten down; to know how much strain his ropes and canvas would stand. And William Nelson knew just that. As a young man he had served his time in the sail-loft. He had seen ships rigged. He had studied the effect of wind and weather on the sails of ships brought into the Ritsons' yard for refit. So that when he took command he knew to a whisker how much punishment his sails and rigging would take.

One of his daughters has recalled how, during every day of a passage, he would climb each mast in turn to examine the state of his gear aloft. How many masters did that? Or, if they had done so, would have had William's understanding of what they saw?

Another example of his thoroughness was the habit, whenever he turned into his bunk, of stowing his clothes in the exact order for putting them on again in darkness if called-out in emergency. This made good sense, for it enabled him to dress rapidly without a lamp and to come on deck with full night vision—a point of great importance: there were no lights on the deck of a Cape Horn windjammer!

But perhaps the supreme example of William Nelson's commonsense is the way he treated his men. Today, an officer's care of the men under his command is something one takes for granted. But not then.

'He always fed his men well,' they said of 'Willie' Nelson. They did not say it of many sailing masters.

At this distance it seems incredible that so much could be put at risk for the sake of a few ounces of food; that ships' masters could starve the very men on whom their own safety and the safety of their ships depended. But they could. And they did. Alan Villiers describes the conditions in a typical 'limejuicer':

The miserable rations as listed were too often made tenfold worse by their appalling quality and the penny-pinching misery with which they were bought, cooked and issued. Much of the bony 'beef' never knew an ox or an ancient cow, though hogs must have been found somewhere of quality bad enough to provide the alleged pork . . .
There was neither leave nor hope of pension for anybody: in far too many ships, not much hope of fair treatment either, and an all-too-prevalent sickening meanness about the miserable food.
    The ship provided no bedding, no bathing facilities nor even eating utensils. Quarters were in a bare steel house on deck, often not warmed by the crudest stove even

in the coldest weather, and vulnerable in a big sea. In this were two rough tables, sometimes with benches to sit at but often not (sea chests were supposed to be used, but at the customary rate of turnover then no foremast hand had a sea chest for long), and a shelflike bunk with a low wooden side to keep the mariner in. These bunks were bare boards; the sailor provided a 'donkey's breakfast' (straw mattress) and a blanket or two, if he joined sober and in funds. This was rare . . . By the grace of God and the humanity born in them, the Learmonts, the Fearons, the Nelsons of Maryport, the Williamses of St Dogmaels, the Jarvises of Tayport, and a good many more never sank to such soul-searing stupidity nor tolerated it when inherited. They were in a minority, unfortunately.*

Claud L. A. Wollard in *The Last of the Cape Horners* cites, among many other miserably sad ships, the barque *Powys Castle* homeward bound from Peru, whose starving crew never got even a drinkable mug of tea or coffee nor properly prepared meal of tolerable food.

It was the cook's practice—by order from the captain—to prepare their tea with the used leaves from the cabin pot thrown in and boiled, and the 'coffee' had a base of inferior beans ground together with burnt ship's biscuit. The bread and biscuits were iron-hard, the beef and pork 'as salt as Lot's wife's ass' and always served half-cooked because, the cook explained, if he cooked it any more it would shrink to nothing. To still their constant pangs of hunger, the sailors ground up grain from burst sacks in the cargo to make watery gruel. They ground the grain with the galley coffee-mill, and were expected to be very grateful for the loan of this.

---

*'The words "Limejuicer" and "Windjammer", the first denoting a British sailing ship and the second any kind of sailing ship, though generally used to describe a square-rigger, were undoubtedly invented by the American sailor, and of the two "Limejuicer" was the first to be broadcast round the world. This word dates from the passing into law of the B.o.T. regulation for the prevention of scurvy, and was invented, I believe, by some contemptuous Yankee after a period of service in a ship where a pannikin of limejuice was served out every day at noon. Thus the word came to denote a ship of British nationality alone, for no other nation instituted this limejuice regulation for its sailors.

The word "Windjammer" does not appear in any of the old nautical dictionaries . . . I am not certain that the American sea writer, T. Jenkins Hains, did not invent it when he put it on the title page of his first book.

At one time it was used a great deal by the officers of steamers, who considered themselves a cut above those who still clung to sail, and was a sneer of contempt in their mouths . . . but the poor old "Windjammer", after being looked upon as a leper of the sea, has in her death-throes come to be regarded by the whole world with admiration and affection, and the term is now no longer one of contempt but of endearment.'

Basil Lubbock. *The Last of the Windjammers*, 1929

Harsh in any age, the conditions of service steadily worsened as the threat of steam became more acute and profits from sailing ships grew more and more slender. But the real reason for this criminal penury, almost always, was that a proportion of the money provided by owners to buy food for the crew found its way into private pockets. Many owners allotted only the barest minimum and any misuse of that money resulted in near-starvation.

Much depended on the ship's master. Some masters were mean to the point of lunacy. There was a master in the four-masted barque *Beechbank*, for instance, who was not just a tyrannical penny-pincher with the food. When sails were repaired and hands were called on to assist himself and the sailmaker, he calculated the amount of sail-twine necessary for each seam and issued that much and no more, so that no one could 'win' enough to sew a button on his pants. When old rags were served out from a bale for paint-washing and the like, he saw that every rag was stabbed with holes, to make sure the sailors couldn't patch old shirts and would have to buy from his slop-chest, at his prices.

There were masters who gave their seamen good canvas and twine enough to make themselves sea-bags, and the wherewithal for eyelets and securing line, too. But the harm done by the stupid was cumulative and, in the end, damaging to the extent that far more was lost than gained, for their miserable penny-pinching was reflected in the slowness of the ship's passage.

In his memoirs, William Nelson writes of that stormy voyage when he took the *Acamas* from Port Talbot round Cape Horn to Pisagua in the dreadful winter of 1905: 'We made the passage out in 109 days, the longest passage I ever made to the West Coast. All the same, it was not so bad comparatively speaking. Some of the ships which left about the same time as us took over 130 days.'

The *Deudrath Castle* never arrived at all. She had sailed on 8th April, 1905 with a cargo of coal from the Tyne for Carrizal in Chile; had a bad time of it off the Horn and eventually, with her cargo heating, turned and put back to Montevideo. There she put her coal ashore to cool off; then re-loaded and sailed for the Horn again.

The weather was just as bad—an endless succession of westerly gales. The ill-fed, ill-housed crew did their best, but rigging damage forced the *Deudrath Castle* back to the Falkland Islands for repairs.

Again she set off for the Horn, and again the gales blew from the west. After a few weeks there was more damage aloft, the coal was heating again and the starving crew were exhausted. Then the eastward bound *Pass of Killicrankie* happened past and offered help. That clinched it. It was 'Abandon ship'!

A lot of ships suffered during that 1905 Cape Horn season. One wonders whether results would have been quite so bad if only those frozen half-starved crews had received just a little more food . . . The *Acamas* faced the same weather, the same gale-force winds; but she got through, and in good time, despite a shifting cargo and smashed hatches.

Almost invariably the sailing ship's tradesmen, or 'petty officers', especially the sailmaker and the carpenter, showed high attention to duty. These were the skilled men. Both had served seven-year apprenticeships before going to sea, for their work was vital. They were privileged people aboard a well-run ship and often the master's friends. They usually shared a tiny cabin amidships and took their meals in the galley.

It was a fool who ill-treated them. But some masters did. The *Claverdon*'s log is a depressing account of crew troubles badly dealt with. Refusals of duty, striking of mates, desertions, replacements by unqualified 'crimp's men' and 'mutiness conduck' (the master's spelling). The sailmaker—ordinarily one of a sailing ship's most loyal servants—became so incensed by the brutality and callous ill-treatment that he 'struck the master to the effusion of blood.'

Log after log among those surviving tells much the same sad story. One wonders how some of the latter-day sailing ships' masters ever attained their position. Certainly, many of them were unfitted for command.

Captain Kennedy of the four-masted barque *Jordanhill*, investigated by the Hong Kong Mercantile Marine Office after constant crew trouble during a two-year voyage between 1904 and 1906, was found to have kept the crew on short rations for eighty-four days by the use of false weights. He was ordered to 'make compensation at the rate of 1d a day to each crew member'. A penny a day!

Some masters, perhaps, were mentally ill. Some tried to do something for their crews, discovering that shortages were sometimes their own fault. In the four-masted barque *Simla*, Captain G. T. Casson logs: 'The crew are complaining at not getting their whack.' He found that the steward had been stealing most of the rations. False weights again.

Planned short delivery aboard against falsified bills in port was a deeper cause of complaint. This fiddling could not be carried through simply by crooked stewards. It was a trick of the trade, a manipulation at the expense of seamen over many years. Most of these rackets were kept out of sight by rapid turnover of crews. Half-starved men melted away as soon as they touched port. Sailors' boarding-house keepers and other 'crimps' saw to that.

The effect of the appalling diet on crew morale cannot be overstressed. Captain William Lord in his book *Real Life at Sea*, published in 1913, had this to say: 'When I first went to sea, food was mostly of the poorest description, and in many cases was absolutely unfit for human consumption . . . it used to be a trite saying on board ship that the Lord sent grub, but the devil cooks. This was in many cases all too true, and more discontent was created on board ship from ill-cooked food than from any other cause.'

William Nelson knew better than to starve his crew. He had known what it was like to be hungry. There was the time he sailed to the Far East as sailmaker/AB in the *James Jardine*, suffering 'fever and leaks and terrible food'. The salt beef, he recalls: 'was as hard as teak. The pork a greasy mass of blubber, the hardtack made from mixed flour and bone-dust and full of maggots. As sailmaker I shared a small wooden compartment secured over a hatchway with the cook, with no bunks or anything.' When he attained

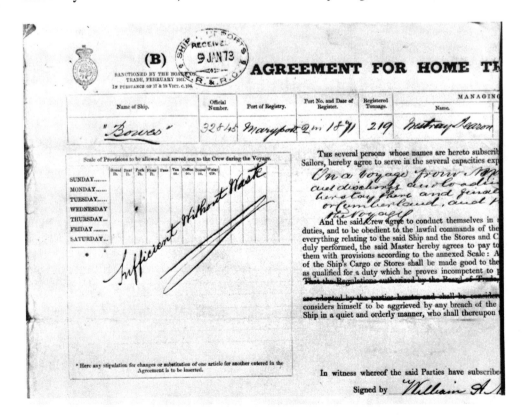

(AC)
SANCTIONED BY THE BOARD OF TRADE, MARCH 1866.
IN PURSUANCE OF 17 & 18 Vict. c. 104.

REGISTER & RECORD OFFICE OF SEAMEN — RECEIVED APR 24 1866

AGREEMENT

, Any Erasure, Interlineation, or Alteration in this Agreement will be void, unless attested

Name of Ship.	Official Number.	Port of Registry.	Port No. and Date of Register.	Registered Tonnage.
"Bowes"	32845	Maryport	15 in 1863	247

Scale of Provisions to be allowed and served out to the Crew during the Voyage.

	Bread lb.	Beef lb.	Pork lb.	Flour lb.	Peas pt.	Tea oz.	Coffee oz.	Sugar oz.	Water qts.
SUNDAY	1	1½	"	½	"	⅛	½	2	3
MONDAY	1	1¼	1¼	"	⅓	⅛	½	2	3
TUESDAY	1	1½	"	"	"	⅛	½	2	3
WEDNESDAY	1	"	1¼	"	⅓	⅛	½	2	3
THURSDAY	1	1½	"	½	"	⅛	½	2	3
FRIDAY	1	"	1¼	"	⅓	⅛	½	2	3
SATURDAY	1	1½	"	"	"	⅛	½	2	3

Here any stipulation for changes or substitution of one article for another may be inserted.

"Substitutes"
Beef and Pork may be substituted for each other
Flour Rice and Peas for each other
One oz of Coffee for ¼ oz of Tea & Vice Versa
One lb of Potatoes for ½ lb of Flour
One lb of Beef or Pork per day and 1 lb of butter per Week may be substituted for 1½ lb of Beef or 1¼ lb of Pork per Day

The several Persons whose names are he… to serve on board the said Ship, in the several cap…

Maryport (via Belfast an…

And the said Crew agree to conduct themse… to the lawful Commands of the said Master, or … and Cargo thereof, whether on board, in boats, o… Wages the Sums against their Names respectivel… or wilful or negligent Destruction of any part of… Person enters himself as qualified for a duty whic… the Regulations authorized by the Board of Trade…

are adopted by the parties hereto, and shall be … aggrieved by any breach of the Agreement or o… thereupon take such steps as the case may require:

In witness whereof the said parties have sub…

Signed by George …

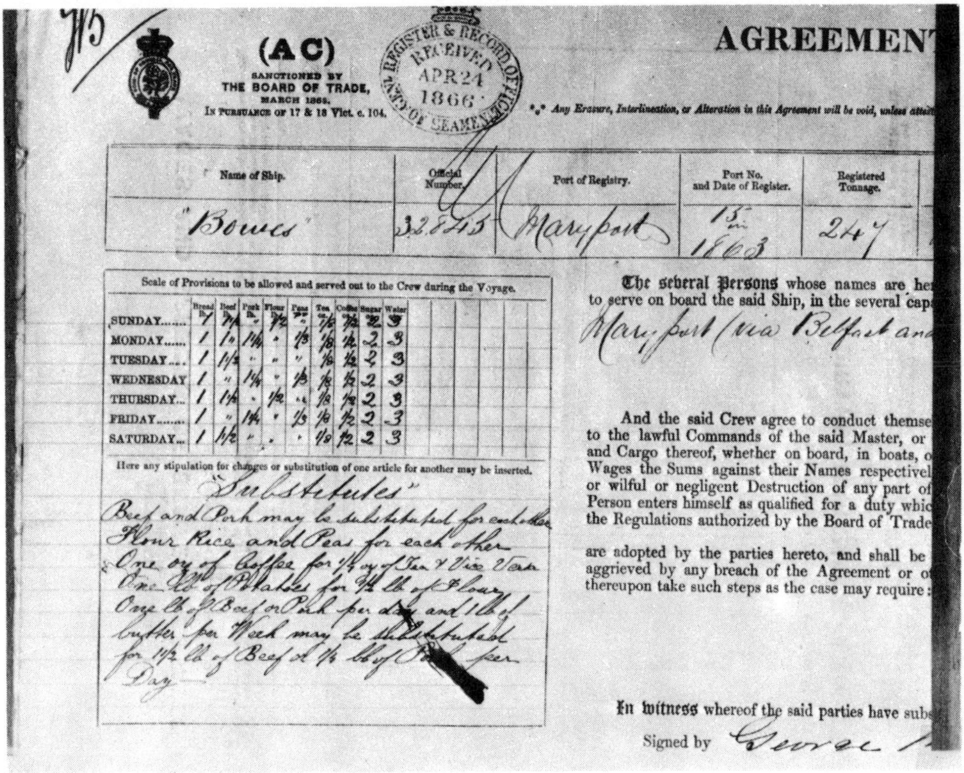

As was the practice in nearly every ship, the master of the Brig *Bowes*—later to be commanded by William Nelson—has given (in 1866) details of the crew's daily rations: bread, beef, pork, flour, peas, tea, coffee, sugar and even water, with substitutes that could be made entirely at the master's discretion; (rations which, in so many ships, were made much worse by their appalling quality).

As seen in the picture opposite, William Nelson would have none of this. 'Sufficient without waste' is what he has written in the Articles of the same ship when he was her master in 1873. And this is what he always gave his men. He had their trust, for in signing-on they accepted that statement for what it was worth. William's care for his crews never changed. Nearly thirty years later, in the Articles of the full-rigged ship *Acamas* we find a similar 'agreement'.

command there was going to be nothing like that. He knew the folly of such penny-pinching; he had seen the results.

In that 1905 winter that saw the end of so many ships, when William sailed the *Acamas* round Cape Horn to Pisagua three weeks faster than most of the others—a voyage that included sheltering for several days in the lee of Staten Island off Tierra del Fuego from an extra savage gale—he saved his men from frostbite by having a tub of straw lashed beside the wheel for the helmsmen to stand in. Later, during a hurricane, he records: 'The two best helmsmen were kept at the wheel, getting a small tot of rum periodically to warm them . . . A high, dangerous sea swept the main deck as the ship staggered along about twelve knots under lower topsails . . .'

The *Acamas* took a tremendous beating. The decks were swept clean of everything movable. The main hatch stove-in. The pumps damaged . . . eight feet of water in the wells. But William brought her safely through. He had a loyal crew. The *Acamas* suffered none of the troubles that filled the logs of so many other ships during that bitter Cape Horn winter.

'He looked after his men *all* the time', they said of him. 'Both in dock and at sea.' And it was true. His roots were in the port whose ships he sailed, and townsmen he knew sailed with him. Men like that fine old Maryport seaman Joseph Monaghan, who served under him for ten years, first as AB and then Bo'sun, and rated him Number One, both from the point of view of his navigating qualities and his treatment of his crews.

But all this was far in the future. At the start of his career, from 1854 to the end of 1861, while his brother Benjamin served his time in the *Hazard*, William was stitching topsails in the Ritsons' Maryport sail-loft.

We may wonder why William's apprenticeship took as long as seven years. But the sailmaker's job was highly skilled, and just what it entailed is made clear in *Sails and Sailmaking* (12th edition, 1887) by Robert Kipping of Newcastle.

Sailmaking demanded a sound knowledge of basic mathematics and practical geometry; an understanding of the principles of drawing and the reading of plans; familiarity with all types of sailing rigs and their running gear, together with the various knots, whippings and splices. Canvas was valuable, no waste was ever permitted. The sailmaker had to calculate the exact amount needed for each type of sail, and be able to find the sail's centre of effort, centre of gravity and moment of force. (Sails, while differing in size according to their type, also differed in size when of the same type but set on different masts—fore, main, mizzen, jigger, etc. They included the courses, topsails, topgallantsails, royals, skysails, moonrakers and other 'moonsails', ringtail and bonnets; all the studdingsails, staysails and jibs; driver, crossjack-sail and many others, each of which had its own rules for determining how each part of it was constructed.) He would also have to calculate hammock-cloths and nettings; awnings of all types; anything, in fact used at sea made of rope and twine and canvas.

The sailmaker was as important to the windjammer as the engineer to the steamer. It was largely on the strength and quality of his handiwork that the ship's speed and safety depended. It mattered little how skilful a ship's master might be at 'carrying-on' canvas if his sails blew out in a wind-strength that should simply have ensured a speedy passage!

As always, Britain's commerce depended on her merchant ships which, in turn, depended on the wind. In the booming days of sail, no matter how precarious the living of a poor and too-rapidly expanding population, no competent sailmaker found himself short of work.

By the end of his apprenticeship, William Nelson's future was secure. But for him, stitching canvas was only a means to an end. His eyes had always looked seawards, to the Solway Firth with its tall ships that sailed to the ends of the earth. With them he had made up his mind to go. But not as sailmaker. At least, not for long. It was command he was determined to get. As he wrote in his memoirs:

'When a boy it was always my ambition to go to sea and become the master of a sailing ship.'

A few years' service before the mast to start with—just long enough to get his time in—then, qualify for second mate. After that, first mate. This was the ladder every future ship's captain had to climb before getting the chance to sit his master's examination and become eligible for command.

William Andrew Nelson, it seems, always knew exactly where he wanted to go, and at times those seven years in the sail-loft must have seemed like eternity. But he was no fool. He recognized the value of what he was learning. By nature he was highly professional in everything he did, and his sailmaking was no exception. In after years his skill with a needle became legendary. As members of his crews claimed: 'He was the best man when it came to sewing up wounds at sea'!

In December, 1861, his indentures with the Ritsons were finalized and he was free to go. But Cumbria at that time did not offer the opportunity he wanted. He headed south to Liverpool. Here was more chance of getting a job afloat, and it was here that his sea-going career began. In the following account of it, based on his memoirs, preserved by his son Captain James Nelson, we accompany him ship by ship, voyage by voyage, as he climbs towards the peak of his profession—and a rightful place in maritime history.

4

The Memoirs of Captain William Andrew Nelson

The *Imperatrice*

In January, 1862, I shipped as sailmaker and A.B. in the auxiliary barque *Imperatrice*, a composite vessel commanded by Captain George Sharp of Maryport. She was at Liverpool loading a general cargo for New York.

The American Civil War was in progress at this time, and owing to a U.S. warship having taken two Government agents belonging to the Southern States from a British Mail steamer, relations became strained between the British and U.S. Governments. For a time it was feared that war might ensue, consequently our loading was stopped until the affair was settled. During this time, Captain Sharp was sent to take charge of another vessel. I don't remember the name of his successor.

We eventually sailed, but had not got very far west of the Fastnet when we fell in with strong westerly gales and a high confused sea. The ship rolled violently and shipped a great deal of water. This did considerable damage to the deck fittings, and after losing the bulwarks we put back to Queenstown* for repairs.

At Queenstown we berthed at a place called 'Passage', lying third ship off from the wharf. It was here, one dark night, that my early sea career nearly came to an end. Going ashore in almost total darkness to post my letters, I crossed the various gangways of the other ships and, alighting on the wharf, thought I was safe. But I had not walked far when I fell over the opposite side of the wharf into the water. Although I was a good swimmer my heavy clothes and boots proved a handicap and it was with difficulty that I managed to keep afloat and hold my own against the tide. Fortunately one of the ships' watchmen had heard the splash and came to my help. After what seemed an age to me in the icy water he succeeded in throwing me a rope and got me back to the wharf. I went back to the *Imperatrice* and turned in, making no further attempts at going ashore in the dark!

Repairs to the ship completed, we sailed and had a fair passage across the

*Now Cobh, south east Eire.

Atlantic with only one day of bad weather—a N.E. gale and blizzard; the coldest day I ever remember.

At New York, government agents tried to persuade the crew to desert and join the American Navy by offering big bounties. But none of us did so.

The passage home was uneventful—except for a fire, which broke out in the after end of the ship. Part of the poop deck had to be cut away to get out some burning bales of cotton. These were thrown overboard and the fire extinguished.

William Nelson's casual reference to the passage home being uneventful 'except for a fire' is typical of the understatement throughout his memoirs. Fire aboard ship has always been one of the most dreaded dangers of life at sea, especially in windjammers with their great quantity of inflammable sails and gear.

Coal in particular was a dangerous cargo. Coal can react with air to produce heat even when it is cold. Normally this is unimportant as it is a very slow process and the heat is readily lost to the surroundings. Some coals, however, have quite high reaction rates. If these are stored in bulk as small pieces or dust with a high surface area exposed, and if air has access to coal in the middle of the store away from the surface so that the heat produced cannot escape, the heat raises the temperature of the surrounding coal. On occasions this process can continue until the temperature is high enough for combustion to occur spontaneously.

In 1875, a Royal Commission was appointed to make inquiry with regard to the causes of the spontaneous combustion of coal in ships—so many vessels having been lost. Indeed, between 1875 and 1883, 57 coal-laden ships were sunk by the firing of their cargoes. During the same period, no less than 328 ships similarly laden were reported missing.

5

The *James Jardine*

On arrival at Liverpool all hands were paid off, having been away about three months. I did not go home to Maryport, but again stayed with my relations until I found another ship.

Keeping abreast of the news while seeking his next job, William may have been amused to read that a member of the House of Lords saw with disgust 'the day when the crew of a warship will be reduced to engineers, stokers and a few artillerymen.' The debate whether the British Admiralty should have iron ships in future received a jolt by a report from the American civil war in April, 1862:

> The combat of the *Merrimac* and the *Monitor* is the subject of comment among several of the Paris journals all of which seem to agree on one point—that a new era of maritime warfare has been inaugurated, and the reign of plain wooden vessels is at an end. The superiority of the iron-cased vessels is so great, that it would be madness, our French contemporaries affirm, to persist in employing ordinary ships of war, when the rush of an iron-covered vessel would crush them like an egg-shell . . . American and French newspapers are crying out: 'Behold, the end of British Maritime Power!'

British Military Power, too, was given some stick. According to another thoughtful editorial:

> A report was presented to the House of Commons last week that reflects anything but well upon the general management of our army in camp. Almost every soldier in the British Army passes through Aldershott once in the year. This season the drunkard and the profligate look forward to with delight, and the prudent with horror and disgust. It is calculated that every man, on an average, has five hours daily to himself; this time he has no opportunity of employing, except in a beer-house or the brothel. The new village of Aldershott is inhabited almost entirely by publicans and prostitutes. The authorities have never, upon any occasion, interfered; yet visible to the eye of every passer-by are scenes of debauchery and drunkenness such as can be witnessed at no other place. The

tavern-keepers are supposed to protect a vile lot of women, that are ever on the watch for opportunities to rob and ruin the young soldier. The very admissions to the hospital prove this fact.

Is it nothing (to set aside the physical loss to the country), is it nothing, we say, that thousands of men should be daily led into unnecessary temptation, that takes them along the wide path of ruin?

Reading this, William Nelson, who was neither drunkard nor profligate, may have congratulated himself on his chosen profession. But the Authority of that time had no more interest in the welfare of its sailors than of its soldiers, although both were indispensable to the country's future.

Even at the peak of its mid-19th-century prosperity, indifferent to the millions of its subjects who lived in poverty and degradation, Britain condoned the miseries of the work-house; the horrors of the treadmill, the whip, the public gallows. And as William soon discovered, even during the days when sail was at its zenith, years before the competition of steam forced windjammer-owners to cut their costs, to reduce and starve their crews, conditions in a merchant ship at sea could be as degrading and dreadful as any suffered ashore.

In the spring of 1862 I joined the wooden ship *James Jardine* as sailmaker and A.B. She was laden with a cargo of coal and bound from Liverpool to Aden round the Cape of Good Hope.

We had not been at sea for many days before I discovered that the *James Jardine* was a most ill-found and hard-case packet. In fact the worst of my whole seafaring experience, as proved in later years. Thirteen wooden casks stowed on deck contained the total fresh water supply, not sufficient to last half the passage. Future deficiencies were made good, when the opportunity occurred, by catching rainwater as it ran from the poop deck. This gave our drinking water a most disagreeable taste!

The food was of bad quality and the rations small, whereas lime-juice was non-existent. The salt beef was all lean, and as hard as teak wood. The salt pork was just a greasy mass of blubber. The hardtack (biscuits), well flavoured with maggots and concocted of a mixture of flour and bone-dust.

As for the accommodation, this was miserable in the extreme. I and the Irish cook shared a small wooden compartment, or 'house', secured over a hatchway. There were no bunks fitted, so I made a couple of canvas hammocks. The state of the ship's gear was just as bad.

A long spell of strong head winds was experienced in the 'Bay' and on a dark night, when all hands were aloft furling the mainsail, a fine young Scotchman fell from the yard through the breaking of a rotten gasket [a gasket is a short length of light rope for making the sail fast to the yard when furled]. He was never seen again.

Looking back on that unhappy voyage I have often wondered that more of us never fell from aloft on the *James Jardine*, as she had single topsails fitted with the Cunningham patent reefing gear.

This patent was rather too complicated to describe in detail, but in brief it amounted to the topsail yard being suspended in the bight of the chain topsail tie or haulyard, the chain tie worked in a whelped grooved boss round the centre of the yard. On each side of the boss were sling hoops within which the yard revolved freely. The sling hoops were attached to the parrall to hold the yard to the mast and yet not to prevent it revolving. There were two sheaves in the masthead through which the two ends of the chain-tie led and a separate set of haulyards fitted to each. To hoist the sail both haulyards were hauled on until as high as the reef bands; then one haulyard was belayed, and by hoisting on the other the yard revolved unfurling the reef. To reef the sail one haulyard only was lowered, the yard revolved and thus reefed the sail. The centre cloth of the sail was cut out from the head to the reef band to allow the sail to roll closely to the yard and not interfere with the revolving whelped boss. A 'bonnet' was substituted for the missing centre-cloth when the sail was fully set.

APPENDIX.

CUNNINGHAM'S PATENT SELF-REEFING TOPSAILS,

FOR

REEFING FROM THE DECK WITHOUT SENDING MEN ALOFT.

Every one, who is at all familiar with maritime matters, will be aware of the great danger attending the operation of reefing topsails in heavy weather by the usual mode of men laying-out on the yards, and gathering up and confining the sail thereto by reef-points and earings, and that fearful accidents are of frequent occurrence on such occasions.

Mr. Cunningham's plan of reefing from the deck purposes to mitigate these dangers; and, from the very favourable reports of a large number of intelligent captains, who have tested the system and experienced great benefits from it, there is every reason to believe that Mr. Cunningham has been successful in the accomplishment of the object which he had in view, by his laudable and ingenious invention becoming generally adopted, particularly among the merchant marine.* The sail can be close-reefed in heavy weather by *one man and a boy, in two seconds and a half*—an operation which, under the

---

* Cunningham's patent is now all the wear. Captains are seeing the utility of it at all times, and merchants are finding the advantage of it, by sending less hands to sea. Although some of our vessels have chafed and worn out a "bonnet" in one voyage of fourteen or fifteen months, yet by a little pains of making a *last* in the sides of the Patent Middle Cloth, when part of the sides get chafed out (for there is plenty of soap used about them), you cut a 12-inches gore in the half breadth, or a right-angle triangle, and *back-stitch* all that part of the tabling which covers the rope, so that the travellers work up and down easily; the back-stitching must be done *well* and *neatly*, and the last being made with a gore, does not lay over on its own part; for if the last is made straight, it will be too thick for the travellers to work over. When the bonnet only is chafed or worn out, shift a new one in its place, and there will be a saving of the cost of bonnet complete, and the labour of sewing the middle cloth into the sail again.

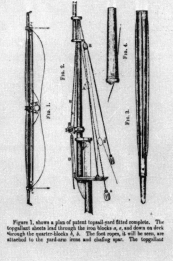

I had thought that William must have been mistaken when he quoted 2½ seconds as the inventor's time for reefing a topsail by man and boy. Merely to loosen or make fast a halyard would take longer than this. But he was right. The facsimile above shows pages from a 19th century sailmaker's manual—a publication William must undoubtedly have studied.

The yard revolved within the yard-arm hoops in the same way with fittings for the stun'sail booms, etc. The idea of this patent was to reduce the number of hands required to reef a topsail in heavy weather. According to the inventor, a man and a boy could reef a sail in 2½ seconds—thus not only reducing the time usually taken, sometimes half an hour or more, but avoiding the danger of men being thrown off the yard. Fine, in theory.

To furl the sail was quite another matter. What with the revolving yard and various gadgets attached, we found it to be a most dangerous operation.

Not long after the loss of the young Scotchman I had a very strange experience. One night as we lay becalmed in the doldrums I dreamt that I was in a ship's cabin talking to my uncle, Captain Jonathan Nelson, although I had not seen him for some time, nor even been thinking of him.

The following morning several ships were in sight and one came close enough to signal. I could not interpret the hoists, not having access to the code book, but it seemed that the other ship was requesting us to send our boat across. She had left home a fortnight after us and promised us some late newspapers.

I left my sail bench to give a hand to get the boat overside, and she was about to shove off in charge of Mr Hurst the second mate, with four seamen, when the mate told me to jump in and keep her baled out.

Distance is deceptive at sea and it was a long pull before we got to the other vessel. I recognised her as the *Uca* of Workington; but even so, had no idea of the master's name.

The second mate went on board and later returned with a bundle of papers. The captain came with him to the poop rail and asked if there was anyone from Cumberland in the boat. To my astonishment it was my uncle Jonathan. He invited me on board, and by a very strange coincidence I found myself in the same cabin and talking to the same man I had dreamt of the previous night!

We chatted about half-an-hour on family affairs when the mate reported 'a breeze making'. Captain Nelson was very kind to me and I felt sorry to have to get back into the boat and return to the *James Jardine*.

Shortly afterwards a good breeze arrived. The *Uca* went ahead and soon passed out of sight.

During the run through the Trade winds I had been employed as a 'day' man, that is working at my bench from 6 a.m. to 6 p.m., making and repairing sails. This of course had meant my getting all night in bed. But now that we were getting well south towards the latitudes of the 'Westerlies', I was taken off day work and put on 'watch and watch' to assist the crew in working the ship.

At this stage of the voyage the captain and officers seemed to be getting more and more afraid of the ship. The rumour was that at some time in the past the *James Jardine* had been aground and broken her back, and now the fear was that in the first heavy weather she would go to pieces! Why the captain had waited until now to worry about this, nobody explained. But there was something on his mind, for soon after this he put the ship about and set a course for Rio Janeiro. He held her in this direction for three days, during which the mate tried to induce the crew to refuse to go on to Aden, our port of destination, on the grounds that the ship was unseaworthy. This would have been tantamount to mutiny and none of us would entertain such an idea. As bad as conditions in the ship were, we preferred to do our duty rather than go to jail at Rio! Without more ado we laid aft and told the captain that if he put into Rio it would be his own responsibility.

After this the ship was again put on her proper course for the 'Cape'. But although we had a good sailing breeze the captain kept the ship under snug canvas, when she should have been doing her best days' sailing.

Not long after this a very curious incident occurred.

One dark night, when there was a fair wind but a heavy following swell, I was startled to hear the mate roar out for all hands to 'lay aft and clear away

The *Southerfield* on the stocks in Ritsons' yard, 1881. The last wooden vessel built at Maryport, she is nearly ready to be launched sideways into the River Ellen, the narrow strip of water bottom right.

Launching of the *Point Clear*.

Maryport waterfront *c.* 1890. The Queen's Head Inn is now the town's maritime museum.

Maryport in Victorian days.

Three topsail schooners in tow outward bound from Maryport, *c.* 1890. In the nineteenth century, small trading vessels such as these were built by private enterprise in nearly every coastal town and village.

The salvage of the damaged four-masted barque *Hougomont* which ran aground north of Maryport, February 1903, by the tugs *Cruiser* and *Wrestler*.

Hougomont safely berthed in Maryport harbour.

The *Auchencairn* under full sail.

The *Auchencairn* at anchor.

The first *Oceanic*, built by Harland and Wolff of Belfast for Thomas Ismay's Ocean Navigation Company. Upon her arrival in the Mersey on February 6th 1871 the *Oceanic* created a sensation. 'More like an imperial yacht than a passenger steamer' it was said of her. In New York she was inspected by over 50,000 people.

Auxiliary schooner *Henry Scholefield* 622 tons, owned by Hines of Maryport, built by S. L. Thompson in 1872.

William Andrew Nelson, photographed in Maryport by Samuel Bettoney, *c.* 1875.

Captain Nelson and his wife, Jane: Quebec, *c.* 1881.

Captain Robert Dixon, photographed in San Francisco about 1880.

Captain John 'Seadog' Jackson of Whitehaven (1799–1879) a highly successful ship's master and iron disciplinarian, allowed no alcohol on board. But perhaps he was not quite so grim as he looks. His wife, Sarah Jopson from Rosthwaite, is said to have had great beauty and charm. Captain Jackson's family was well known to the Nelsons.

Seaman John Leece, associate of Captain W. A. Nelson, photographed at the age of 95.

the boats and abandon ship'! When I got aft the carpenter (chips) was sitting on the spanker boom, very excited and crying like a child, while the captain dressed only in his shirt and drawers was cutting away the lashings on the ship's gig. When I asked him what was the trouble, he shouted: 'Clear away this boat! Don't you know the ship is sinking?'

By this time everyone had laid aft, but while the panic party was busy clearing the sea-lashings from the boats, one of the sailors—who was taking things very coolly—asked me to go with him to sound the wells. He said he thought it strange for the ship to be sinking, as they had only just pumped her dry during the dog watch! Sure enough, on sounding the wells we found only a few inches of water. And when we reported this to the captain and the two mates things gradually became normal again.

Whether this scene had been staged I never found out. More likely it was due to sheer incompetence. From the evidence of the helmsman it appeared that the ship was making little headway owing to the small amount of sail set, and while the mate was lighting his pipe by the companion scuttle, the ship's stern dipped into an extra heavy swell and a sluice of water, rushing up the wide rudder trunk, nearly washed the mate off his feet. He immediately shouted down to the captain to hurry on deck as the ship was sinking! This the captain had done in quick time. But he took no steps to ascertain the truth of the mate's assertion, hence the panic.

What a sad and sorry picture the *James Jardine* presents. An ineffectual master; weak officers; an ill-fed and ailing crew.

What might have happened I wonder, after that wave sluiced up the rudder-trunk and splashed the mate, if the only cool-headed sailor on board had not suggested to William Nelson that they sound the wells? Supposing the crew *had* taken to the boats (whose lashings were already being cut) and subsequently, as was quite likely, been overcome by bad weather before being rescued or making land. What then, with no one left to tell the tale, if some passing ship's crew had found the *James Jardine* staggering along, and boarded her—as the *Marie Celeste* was to be found and boarded on 5th December, 1872? Her abandonment for no apparent reason would surely have been regarded as another of those 'Inexplicable Mysteries of the Sea'—which in time inspire a host of articles and books! And all because of a timid and probably drunken master together with a mate who panicked and lost his head.

Of such material were many sea mysteries undoubtedly made.

All in all another lucky escape for William Nelson. And he was lucky in other ways. Experience is fine, provided one survives to profit from it—as

William did; although, on the *James Jardine*'s interminable voyage in 1862, matters went from bad to worse.

After rounding the Cape of Good Hope one of the sailors took seriously ill. No one knew what ailed him, but he got so bad that he went out of his mind. The captain ordered me to make a strait-jacket for him, and after about a week of this the poor fellow died. I was the only one on board having a prayer-book, which I lent to the captain to read the burial service.

I forgot to mention that when I returned to our 'hutch' after the panic episode, I found the Irish cook all dressed up in his Sunday 'best'. He told me that the last time he had to abandon ship he had only his working clothes on. This time he was making sure to save his best.

We eventually arrived at Aden in September, the hottest month of the year, after a long passage of 147 days. Four of the crew were down with scurvy.

Our lot at Aden was not a happy one. We were still on poor food and fresh vegetables were unobtainable. So much time was lost in discharging the cargo and taking in ballast that, by the time we had finished, the N.E. monsoon had set in. This meant another long passage—to Akyab, our next port of call.

After a passage of 84 days we arrived at Akyab with most of the crew ill with scurvy and the remainder almost too weak to work. Our combined strength was not sufficient to raise the anchor, and before we could get underway to proceed to our berth the captain sent the pilot ashore to bring off a gang of coolies to work the ship into port.

At Akyab the captain took to drinking, and neglected business. He got so bad that at last he was dismissed, and the mate took over command. But matters got steadily worse. We were all more or less ill, and so discontented that we demanded an official survey of the ship's provisions—and requested to be paid off, as none of us desired to proceed farther in such a ship.

Eventually, a Court of Enquiry was held before the magistrate, an old army officer, who held that the provisions be condemned and those desirous to be paid off.

The finding of the magistrate's Court of Enquiry says all that need be said about the conditions aboard the *James Jardine*. For officialdom to give such unqualified support to the complaints of a sailing ship's crew—and about food, of all things—was exceptional. Needless to say, the crew received only a part of the money due to them—although doubtless they thought themselves lucky to get anything. Only William, with the foresight of the dedicated career man, had the patience to ensure his just reward.

We all took our discharge, but only received two months' wages in cash—with a bill on the owners for the balance! We then took passage on a British India steamer to Calcutta where we stayed at the Sailor's Home, paying a month's board in advance. The rest of the crew cashed in their bills for balance of wages with the master of the Home, who charged them 50% on the transaction! But I kept my bill, and although about two years were to elapse before I had the pleasure of presenting it to the Owners in Liverpool I eventually got paid in full. I never heard of or saw the old *James Jardine* again, I fancy she was soon condemned. If not she ought to have been.

While I was in Calcutta I took what was called the 'Country' fever. The local fever hospital was full and could not take me in, so I stayed where I was at the Sailor's Home. I was not laid up with it, but had a constant thirst and no appetite. Anyway, I got over it, and had been at the Home about three weeks when a Captain Kerr of the wood-built ship *Sevilla* came seeking a sailmaker/A.B., and I got the job.

6

The *Sevilla*

After my experience in the *James Jardine* I was glad to sign-on for service in the *Sevilla*. She was a fine, well-found vessel employed in the passenger and emigrant trade. Her master, Captain Kerr, was a gentleman and an excellent seaman. The *Sevilla* had taken emigrants from England to New Zealand and sailed in ballast to Calcutta with the object of taking Coolies to the West Indies, but had arrived too late in the season.

In order to put in time until the next Coolie season, we sailed from Calcutta to Masulipatam and loaded a cargo of peas for Mauritius. Then, after some other coasting voyages, we finally returned to embark the Coolies.

We left Calcutta for Demerara with a few hundred Coolies on board and had a fine and pleasant passage to our destination.

From the West Indies we proceeded to London with a cargo of sugar and rum. Although I had been away from home for about two-and-a-half years I stayed with the ship and, at the request of Captain Kerr, made a coastwise trip to Glasgow, promising to sail with him again on the next voyage.

From Glasgow I took a holiday. But instead of going direct to my home in Maryport I proceeded to Liverpool and gave the owners of the *James Jardine* a little surprise—by presenting my bill for my balance of wages, which by now, was about two years overdue. They paid me in full.

I then went to Maryport and enjoyed a well-earned rest ashore.

During William's holiday, which stretched from the end of 1864 over Christmas into 1865, he would undoubtedly have been interested, and perhaps saddened, to hear that due to the establishment of the Solway Lightship, use of the Salterness Lighthouse—built by his grandfather—was to be discontinued on the expiry of six months from December 23rd. But the proposal for a lighthouse at the end of Maryport's south pier would assuredly have met with his approval. There was also the exciting possibility of a new dock.

This momentous question [wrote Robert Adair in his newspaper] has formed the current topic of town gossip . . . It has been very gracefully conceded on all hands that additional harbour space is imperatively demanded in order to meet the requirements of the vastly increased trade of the port.

At the half-yearly meeting of the Maryport and Carlisle Railway Co., the Chairman, announcing a dividend of 11%, congratulated the shareholders on the very prosperous state of the Company.

Mr Musgrave of Whitehaven, however, objected in strong terms to any portion of the shareholders' capital being devoted to a dock at Maryport. He described the scheme as 'Utopian'.

Among the other items of local news during William's holiday, we find that oysters were plentiful on the nearby beaches.

Some of our Maryport epicures [wrote Robert Adair] have availed themselves of the opportunity of a haul of the aristocratic delicacy. This, we understand, has excited the jealousy of some of the butchers in the neighbourhood, though we do not hear that the take has tended to lower the price of meat.

A local advertisement, however, announced a reduction in the price of tea. Mr F. Walker was offering it at a penny an ounce.

At Christmas, William—who had something of an ear for music—might have been found among the audience of nearly four hundred who 'enjoyed' the Maryport Charity Amateur Dramatic Performance.

Of the merits of this entertainment [reviewed the *Maryport Advertiser*] we are disposed to speak with tenderness; although a little wholesome criticism may prove of service to the actors on some future occasion.

A more sombre note was struck by 'Town Scavenger', who wrote:

Sir—I have observed recently that the nuisance committee have brought before the Trustees several offences of a comparatively trivial character compared with the wholesale nuisance which, if not checked in the beginning will extend throughout the town and most likely will land us in as fearful a visitation of fever as lately devastated Whitehaven. I allude to the converting of old wells in and near to dwelling houses into cesspools and water closets. When the government commissioner visited Whitehaven to investigate the cause of the malignant fever that caused such great mortality in that town, he reported that the old wells which had been superseded by the introduction of waterworks had been ever since used as water closets and reservoirs of all sorts of filth . . . If the nuisance committee will make enquiry in this town, they will find that the foul practice which brought such calamity to Whitehaven has been commenced here. If not prevented in time we need not wonder at the result.

The result was typhoid fever. But, by then, William was far away at sea in the *Sevilla*.

> It would be in 1865 that we sailed from the Clyde with passengers and a general cargo for New Zealand. The passage out was fine and pleasant, except for the usual gales when running the Easting down, and we arrived at Bluff Harbour some 96 days out.
>
> In those days there was only one suitable wharf where a deepwater ship could safely birth. The town consisted of a few wooden houses and tents, and we discharged one of the first consignments of railway material for building the line from Bluff Harbour to Invercargill.
>
> At Bluff Harbour, much to my regret, Captain Kerr was taken out of the *Sevilla* in order to take command of the *Arima*, another of the same company's vessels. He was replaced by Captain Smith.
>
> We sailed from Bluff Harbour in ballast for Hong Kong, and made rather a long passage. Unlike our recent captain, Captain Smith did not believe in carrying sail, and at sundown no matter how fine and settled the weather he had all small sails furled for the night.

William Nelson's sense of frustration can readily be imagined. He had seen the result of unnecessary snugging-down when in the *James Jardine*. It was a mistake he was never to make himself. In later years, when he gained command and became famous for his fast passages—made not in clippers but run-of-the-mill work-ships—he carried sail as hard by night as by day, coming on deck at all hours to check a change in weather like any ocean-racing yachtsman of today. But many masters were inclined to be over-cautious.

Captain Maitland, who commanded the 2,270-ton steel ship *Valkyrie*, was a great believer in safety-first. After latitude 50 S., he would order every sail to be reefed before being furled. This was not popular with the crew, since it meant they were aloft for double the time whenever they shortened sail: they called it 'The Old Man's Tuck'. (It was not a squall that sank the *Valkyrie*, but she was lost just the same. Collision, in 1901.)

> At Hong Kong we received orders to proceed up-river to Whampoa and it took us nearly a week to sail there. The ship had been chartered to carry Chinese Coolies to the West Indies. The embarking of these proved a slow process as only one or two junks arrived alongside each day from Canton, carrying men, wives and children.
>
> An interesting but rather trying month was spent at Whampoa. Chinese pirates and thieves were active, which meant that the crew had to be constantly on guard and maintain the strictest vigilance day and night.

We sailed from Whampoa with about 500 Coolies on board bound for Demerara, and soon found the Chinese much more troublesome than the Indians. Our first job was to erect a barricade across the main deck in front of the poop—to prevent the Chinese from suddenly rushing the after end of the ship! A most fortunate and provident act, as events proved.

The Chinese spent their time gambling and grumbling. Their food consisted mainly of rice, pork and fish, and they were continually whining about the size of their rations, especially the fresh water. A Chinaman is a very extravagant individual at any time with fresh water. It was water that caused the first real trouble we had with the Chinese—not fresh water, as it happened, but salt. It all started when the bo'sun was washing-down on top of the forward house. He hove a bucket of water over the long-boat—and drenched a Chinaman who was on the other side washing his clothes.

In the row that followed, the Chink threw his wash-tub at the Bo'sun. Whereupon the Bo'sun grabbed a broom from a sailor and aimed a mighty blow at the Chink's head. Luckily for the Chinaman the force of the blow was broken when the broom caught the foot of the mainsail, but it was a signal for a free-for-all! Other Chinese came running up and joined in the fray and things began to look very serious. Then, not a moment too soon, the mate appeared on the scene with a revolver—and settled the matter for the time being.

Some time later a more serious fight occurred. The Chinese had hung a lot of stinking fish to the ratlines to be sun-dried, and when the watch on deck was laying aloft (most of them in their bare feet) to furl a sail, they cut away the fish. Some of the fish fell on deck, but a lot went overboard. This started a general riot. The Chinese armed themselves with any suitable weapons they could find—belaying pins and marlin spikes mainly—and drove the sailors on deck aft beyond the barricade.

For a time the Chinese had the main deck to themselves and the scene looked very ugly. But when the captain and mates appeared with rifles and cutlasses they all ran below like a lot of rabbits. The captain read the 'Riot Act' and the doctor attended to the injured. After that things became normal again and we had no further trouble.

A doctor on board! This is the only mention anywhere in William's memoirs of such an unlikely member of a windjammer's crew. Presumably, since she occasionally carried passengers, the *Sevilla* was one of those Merchant Ships Required to Carry a Surgeon. In ships handling cargo only, no doctor was carried. While he was on his feet a seaman was presumed fit. No medical certificate was required when he signed-on, his only qualification being a valid Discharge Book, or a Discharge Paper from his last ship.

Even when passengers were carried, a doctor was by no means always a windjammer crew member. From a letter written to his son by Captain John

Rich of the *Brier Holme* (see also, p.86), when in the West India Dock, London, 1904, it is clear that the only doctor aboard his ship was sailing as a private passenger. The news that the doctor's wife is sailing too, is received by Captain Rich without enthusiasm.

> I hear we are to take a Doctor and his wife as passengers (private). I would not mind the Doctor, but a woman without it's your dear mother, I hate to have on board, as they want so much waiting on and there should be a special steward to attend on their *hundred and one* fanciful requirements, which cannot be given to them on board an ordinary 'windjammer' for I only carry a Cabin Boy who wants stirring up every few minutes in the day, and as your dear Mother is not going with me suppose shall have to wash and dress her if the dear Doctor is sick . . . As a rule Lady Passengers are never contented with their rations and the Cooking on board a sailing vessel . . .

Any doctoring at sea was done by the master with the aid of *The Ship Captain's Medical Guide* together with the (usually very sparse) contents of his Medical Chest. Surgery was commonly left to the ship's carpenter or the sailmaker. Injuries caused by falling from aloft rarely caused trouble; they were nearly always fatal! Few sailors who fell overboard were recovered. Head injuries, damaged joints and hands, broken bones—the master did the best he could; the carpenter fashioning splints, the sailmaker stitching cuts. William, who had served his time in sailmaking, was very adroit with needle and palm and in later years, when a master himself, had quite a reputation for cobbling up wounds.

Stomach pains and the like were treated with one of the 'Ten Mixtures' from the Chest, according to instructions in the *Guide*. These were seldom helpful. A dose of 'Black Draught' (a powerful decoction of senna) with advice to keep warm, did nothing for the A.B. on board the *Sofala* who crushed his hand and later complained of 'stiffness of the jaws'. After all, neither Medical Guide nor Chest, nor even a sympathetic master, could cope with tetanus!

1.—*Saline Mixture*		
Bicarbonate of potash	2	drachms
Nitrate of potash	1	drachm
Water	6	oz.
2 tablespoonfuls for a dose.		

2.—*Fever Mixture*		
Nitrate of potash	1	drachm
Sweet spirits of nitre	3	drachms
Spirits of chloroform	1½	drachm
Add water to	6	oz.
2 tablespoonfuls for a dose.		

3.—*Diarrhœa Mixture*

Elixir of vitriol 2	drachms
Laudanum . . . . . ½	drachm
Spirits of chloroform . . 1½	drachm
Add water to 6	oz.

2 tablespoonfuls for a dose.

4.—*Soothing Mixture*

Bromide of ammonium . . 1½	drachm
Spirits of chloroform . . . 2	drachms
Paregoric 1½	drachm
Bicarbonate of soda . . . 1	drachm
Add water to 6	oz.

2 tablespoonfuls for a dose.

5.—*Clap Mixture*
(This must be well shaken.)

Balsam of copaiba . . . 3	drachms
Sweet spirits of nitre 2	drachms
Friar's balsam 1	drachm
Add water to 6	oz.

2 tablespoonfuls for a dose.

6.—*Stomachic Mixture*

Spirits of chloroform . . . 2	drachms
Bicarbonate of soda . . . 2	drachms
Essence of ginger 1	drachm
Add water to 6	oz.

2 tablespoonfuls for a dose.

7.—*Cough Mixture*
(To be well shaken.)

Powdered ipecacuanha . . 12	grains
Paregoric 2	drachms
Sweet spirits of nitre . . . 3	drachms
Spirits of chloroform . . . 2	drachms
Add water to 6	oz.

2 tablespoonfuls for a dose.

8.—*Stimulant Mixture*

Aromatic spirits of ammonia . 3	drachms
Spirits of chloroform . . . 2	drachms
Add water to 6	oz.

2 tablespoonfuls for a dose.

9.—*Quinine Mixture*

Quinine 12	
Elixir of vitriol . . . . ½	drachm
Add water to 6	oz.

2 tablespoonfuls for a dose.

10.—*Witch Hazel Mixture*

Witch hazel (ext. hamamelidis liq.) 1	drachm
Water 6	oz.

1 or 2 tablespoonfuls for a dose.

10 Mixtures from *The Ship Captain's Medical Guide*. This list is from the 14th Edition, published by Simpkin, Marshall, Hamilton, Kent & Co. London, 1906.

But to return to William aboard the *Sevilla*:

For the remainder of the voyage the Chinese spent most of their time gambling away their Government bonuses. Evidently they caught one of the party cheating, for one morning we found a Chinaman trussed up to a spare spar by his pigtail. This spar was stowed on the forward deck house and extended to the fo'c'sle head. During the night they had taken their victim out on deck near the fore-mast and there lashed his wrists together behind his back; then, lifting him up until his head was level with the spar, they passed his pigtail over the spar and down his back and firmly hitched his pigtail to the wrist lashing. There they left him hanging—until we found him in the morning, more dead than alive!

William is silent on the fate of this unfortunate gambler. Whether he was given one of the Mixtures is not recorded.

At St Helena a call was made for fresh vegetables and water. We also took on eight negroes for the run to Demerara.

When the pilot came aboard off Demerara he told us that many seamen from the ships in port were in hospital with Yellow Fever and that a number had died. It appeared that a recent fire, which had devastated the water-front, was responsible for the excavating work now in progress for rebuilding purposes and that this work was blamed for the fever epidemic. A few of our men went to hospital with the fever, but they were lucky enough to recover and rejoin the ship.

After the Chinese disembarked we got the ship cleaned up, and glad we were to get it done. Then we loaded a cargo of sugar and rum for Greenock. Also, a few saloon passengers embarked. We made a good run home.

Our next voyage was a short one. We took a general cargo from the Clyde to the West Indies, and came back to Greenock with the usual cargo of sugar.

My next voyage was out to Rangoon, and back to Liverpool.

I had now put in sufficient sea time to allow me to sit for the first of my examinations. In what little spare time I had had at sea I had done a fair amount of studying, and after a brief spell at school I went up and passed for second mate without any difficulty. This would be about 1867.

I had not long to wait for my next job, being offered the post of second mate in the ship *Empress Eugenie*.

7

The *Empress Eugenie*

The *Empress Eugenie* was a wooden-built ship sheathed with yellow metal and built at Sunderland in 1854 for Messrs Bonus of London. In 1864 she was sold to Messrs Shute of Liverpool. Captain Collins of Maryport held command under her new ownership, and stayed with her until she was again sold, in 1870.

I gladly accepted the offer of the second mate's appointment under my fellow townsman Captain Collins, and on the journey to Milford Haven where I was to join the *Empress Eugenie*, felt proud to think that at last I could take an active part in ship-handling and navigation from the quarter-deck—though when I got on board my enthusiasm suffered a slight set-back. My predecessor, I was casually informed, had been killed by the spanker-gaff falling on him!

One feels that William was being unduly sanguine when, as second mate, he looked forward to taking an active part in the *Empress Eugenie*'s navigation. In many windjammers it was unusual for either of the mates to share in the navigation. All too often, absurd though it may seem, the ship's position was kept the master's secret. The charts (often out of date) were the master's property, and he kept them jealously guarded.

If Captain Collins encouraged William to help in finding and plotting the ship's position, he was out of the usual run of sailing ship's captains. But then, he *was* out of the ordinary, and he almost certainly did share the navigation, for there is no mention otherwise in William's memoirs. After all, they were both Maryport men. And Maryport, for all the fine ships it built and its importance as a seaport, was only a tiny town. Everybody in it connected with the sea would have been 'public property'. William, who had a deep respect for Captain Collins, would have known all about his future captain long before signing on as second mate. (Captain Collins' father was a leading Maryport solicitor.)

Captain Collins was a great driver. At the start of the voyage there were seven spare booms for the stun-sails and he rarely took in one of these sails until the boom carried away! When only three booms remained he became more careful.

We sailed from Milford Haven for Karachi and were not long out when the ship developed a very bad leak, making a constant seven inches of water hourly. This seemed odd, for the ship had recently been in drydock. However, four men had to be told off from each watch on deck to keep the pumps working continuously. This left us with only three A.B.s for handling the ship.

Off Mauritius we fell in with a cyclone and, in order to avoid the centre, the ship was run to the southward for two days. During this time the sky had a very wicked appearance: heavily overcast, lead-coloured with very low fast-moving clouds, which hung over us like a pall. It blew a full gale, with a high and dangerous sea. Not a pleasant situation for a leaky ship. But Captain Collins brought her through with very little damage.

During some calm weather near the 'Line', the captain of another ship came on board by Captain Collins' invitation. He stayed about two hours discussing our strange leak and was as puzzled as we were. We took further soundings, but the ship was still making the same seven inches per hour.

On arrival at Karachi an extra pump was hired, together with a gang of coolies to do the pumping—much to the relief of the sailors who had been at this back-breaking job, watch by watch, for nearly three months.

After the cargo was discharged we discovered the cause of this mysterious leak. Taking advantage of damage to one of the metal strips sheathing the hull marine worms had eaten a hole through the planking! Fortunately, we were able to stop the leak from inside the ship, by caulking and then nailing a piece of sheet lead over it. This saved us from making a long trip to Bombay for inspection, which otherwise we should have had to do, since there was no dry-dock in Karachi.

While still at Karachi I had an experience that very few people can have had and escaped with their lives. On Sunday mornings the mate and I would take it in turn to sail one of the ship's boats to church, and those in the crew who wished to go could do so. One Sunday, the mate having been to church, the boat was free. The Captain had friends on shore, mostly army officers, and was seldom on board on Sundays. So, in the afternoon the steward asked me to take him for a sail.

We got into the boat and hoisted sail. She had a nice suit of sails. But after leaving the ship one of the rudder-irons broke, so of course we couldn't steer very well. I let the boat go before the wind until she ran aground, and there lowered sail, but when we tried to push off under oars the oars stuck in the mud, and in trying to pull them out we simply pulled the boat back on the mud again. This meant we had to get overboard and try to walk her off.

I had only gone a step or two when I felt something under my foot, and on looking down saw to my horror the back of a big snake, as thick as my arm, writhing against my leg. Instantly, I jumped into the boat. So did the steward—in double quick time! The quickest jumps I should think either of us ever made. Fortunately we had got the boat afloat, so that now we could row her off with the oars, which we did very promptly. I must have had my foot on that snake just behind its head, or without doubt it would have bitten me. Most likely I would have been dead before we reached the ship.

There was nothing else worth recording until we were about halfway home. We had left Karachi for Liverpool with a cargo of cotton and rape seed and made good progress until, a little north of the equator, the wind fell away completely. And there we stayed, in one of the longest and most complete calms I ever experienced.

During the first week of calm, Captain Collins kept mostly to his cabin playing the flute, appearing on the poop occasionally to whistle for a breeze.

During the second week however, he abandoned his serenading of King Boreas. With a more practical turn of mind he set the hands to holystoning the decks. He kept them at this from 5.30 am until 5.30 pm with no afternoon watch below. On the Saturday they were kept holystoning until 3 pm, but spent the rest of the day, until dusk, washing down decks, sweating up halyards and braces and overhauling buntlines.

Captain Collins seems to have been somewhat eccentric, but no fool. Clearly, he understood the morale-sapping effect of prolonged inactivity. A week of it was all very well. A pleasant enough interlude in the battle with the sea—and time for some flute practice. But a week was long enough. After that he saw to it that everyone was kept busy.

As a ship-driver he was obviously a man after William's own heart. From him, the future Captain Nelson undoubtedly learned much about over-sailing and under-sailing a ship: that middle course between recklessness and over-caution which later he was to steer so accurately himself. Admittedly, Captain Collins seems to have judged when to shorten sail largely by the strength of his stun'sail booms; but for all that, as his ship-handling proved during the cyclone, like most of his Maryport contemporaries he was an excellent seaman.

Much to everyone's relief a breeze came during the third week and carried us into the S.E. trade wind.

On the run home, which was very pleasant, the usual sailing ship routine work was carried out: holystoning decks, sand and canvassing teak houses and rails, ratlining and tarring down, scraping and varnishing masts and spars, making fancy knots on various lanyards, etc, in order that the ship might look clean and trim on her arrival home.

Approaching our landfall we did a smart bit of 'beating' to windward. Saturday, 4 am, 10 miles off Fastnet, tacked ship to southward. At 8 pm same day, tacked to northward. Sunday, 1 pm, 3 miles off Tuskar Rock, tacked ship to southward. At 8 pm same day, tacked to northward. On the following day (Monday) at 10 am took a tugboat off the South Stack, owing to Easterly winds, and anchored in the Mersey the same night.

After I paid off I went to school in Liverpool and passed my first mate's examination, before going home to Maryport for a holiday.

(Ironically, in 1869 while William Nelson was acquiring his mate's ticket, last stepping-stone towards command of a square-rigger, something happened that in later years did much to put the square-rigger out of business—the opening of the Suez Canal.)

Nowhere in his memoirs does William tell us what he did during his infrequent holidays between voyages, but early in 1870 he could for the first time, if he wished, have caught a train to Cockermouth seven miles away; this branch of the Maryport and Carlisle Railway having been opened in 1867 while he was sailing the China Seas.

For his entertainment there was the annual social tea party of the United Presbyterian Chapel, attended by some two hundred members. There was also a Charity Concert in aid of the Workhouse Children given by the Cockermouth amateurs. He was not a drinking man, so the popular 'Captain's Room' of the Golden Lion Hotel, frequented by ship's masters and officers, would not have seen much of him. Probably, most of his time was spent in Messrs Ritsons' shipyard or on the waterfront, where there was usually plenty of incident. As Frederick Kelly wrote:

It was a great sight to see the fleet of sail ships approaching the port after a long spell of easterly winds. It was first come first served, and the rush for the entrance was exciting in the extreme. As many as eighty-nine vessels have entered in one tide, and 116 in two consecutive tides. Then when the wind had been westerly for a spell, it was which vessel could get away among the first. And there was fun . . . More than sixty vessels were known to get to sea in a single tide. The excitement was great. Vessels jamming in to prevent others getting away. Ropes without number attached to the mooring posts at the Pierheads. The Harbour Master shouting orders to which no heed was given, then calling for an axe and cutting away every rope made fast on the quays. There was 'some' language at such times, for it seemed as though in that way only could the intense excitement spend itself. Often was the old harbour so full of ships that it was possible to cross from the South quay to the North across the vessels.

There was certainly intense excitement in the crowded harbour one night when the schooner *Euphemia* caught fire. 'The flames from her mainsail illuminated the lower part of the town and soon attracted a large crowd.' Fortunately, the tide was in and a holocaust avoided without the aid of the Fire Engine, which was in attendance.

In the Maryport of 1869–70 in spite of constant argument about the town's sanitation, the 'musical carts'* still plied their noisome trade. But the old town pump had stopped clanking, and William would certainly have enjoyed the novelty of the new piped-water system. He was not a man for lingering at home, however; he had a fine new first mate's ticket and (as he said) was eager to get back to sea.

---

*Horse-drawn carts that collected the day's sewage, left by the townspeople in pails and tubs along the streets. A cart's approach was heralded by the ringing of a bell.

8

The *Tinto*

After my holiday in Maryport I returned to Liverpool in search of a first mate's job. Not being able to find one immediately, and in order not to waste time, I shipped as second mate on the full-rigged ship *Tinto* of Glasgow, a wooden vessel sheathed with yellow metal. This would be in 1870.

We sailed from Liverpool with a cargo of salt for Calcutta. The outward passage was uneventful and I can't recall any incidents worth recording.

We sailed from Calcutta with a cargo of jute for Dundee and made a good passage to the chaps of the Channel. There fortune turned against us and we were held up by a prolonged spell of Easterly winds. Nearly another month elapsed before we reached our destination!

While still in the Atlantic and before making land we had exchanged chronometer times with a French ship. Much to our Captain's surprise he found that his time-piece was in error eight minutes: or two degrees of longitude! After this he was very cautious and heaved the ship to each night. When we finally made the land however, and checked the chronometer, we found that our time was not much in error. The Frenchman had reckoned his time from the meridian of Paris—hence the eight minutes of difference between Greenwich and Paris! Had it not been for this ridiculous mix-up we should have made our landfall much sooner and been bowling up the Channel before that period of Easterlies set in. As it was the easterly winds continued and we had plenty of hard work in tacking up-Channel.

It was to avoid such confusion that the international congress at Washington, U.S.A. in 1884 decided to reckon longitude—and thus nautical time—from the meridian of Greenwich. France, however, abstained. Not until 1911 did France finally adjust her measurements and French sailors take their longitude East or West of Greenwich and not Paris.

Even when we reached the North Sea we were no better off, for the wind backed northerly and we continued to make very slow progress. Finally our fresh water gave out and we were forced to put into Grimsby Roads to replenish. There I had a very lucky escape.

To get the fresh water we had to take a ship's boat ashore full of empty casks and fill them from a pump. This meant several trips before we had sufficient. As second mate I was sent in charge of the boat and on the last trip we nearly came to grief. I had turned the boat's head to the tide, forward of the ship, in order to drop down alongside with the current, stem first, but as we did so the ship suddenly broke her sheer due to a fluke of wind, and the cable, rising up suddenly, caught under the keel of our boat, throwing it on its side and half filling it with water. By a piece of great good fortune we got clear without capsizing—which saved us a long swim and, indeed, probably saved our lives, because the water was cold, the current very strong—and the other ship's boats still had their sea lashings on and would have taken many minutes to get out.

Their escape illustrates so well the old axiom that irrespective of location, the sea is never safe. Many a sailor, having survived an ocean passage, has drowned in port. To the unlucky, or ill-prepared, or ignorant, the shoals and tidal currents of the British coast can be as deadly as Cape Horn—as many a yachtsman has found to his cost. William and his boat's crew were neither ignorant nor ill-prepared; they met with a genuine 'accident'. To avoid a backbreaking, perhaps impossible row in a heavily laden boat against the strong Humber current, they wisely headed out from the shore upstream of the *Tinto* and finished up ahead of the ship, so that they could drop down stern-first with the tide. Then—a sudden shift of wind makes the ship swing and tighten on her cable, which rears up from beneath the surface like a bar of iron . . . ! At moments such as these Chance truly plays its part, when a few inches one way or the other determine the difference between life and death.

We got to Dundee eventually. There I paid off and went to Maryport for a short holiday. After a pleasant relaxation I went to Liverpool to sit for master.

I passed my examination on the 2nd October, 1871, Certificate No. 85903.

Being well advanced with the work, I had put my papers in to sit for Extra-master, but the Examiner told me to come up at a later date as it was his rule to grant 'Extra' certificates only to those who had been in command for at least twelve months.

After this I never bothered to sit again.

There was no reason why he should have done. An extra-master's ticket offers no extra powers. It is simply a sort of mariner's PhD—a useful qualification for marine jobs ashore, but of no particular purpose to William, whose eyes were set for ever seaward.

It is interesting that until the middle of the last century neither master nor mate needed formal qualifications. In many ships, position-finding was primitive; vessels were still being navigated by latitude sailing, and although the chronometer and nautical almanac were products of the 1760s, few attempts were made to calculate longitude.

In the second half of the century a more rigorous approach was adopted towards the training of ship's officers. By 1888, for example, the Board of Trade standards required that a second mate be no younger than seventeen, but with four years at sea—so that going to sea at the age of thirteen was envisaged! The second mate, furthermore, had to be capable of finding his latitude from meridian altitude, and his longitude from sun sights and chronometer. (Many a second mate 'made up' at sea in emergency was unable to do any of that. In 1907 on the voyage of the *Ladas*, William is forced to alter course for Monte Video when—with an insane first mate and uncertificated second mate—he finds himself the only navigator on board.)

Although I now had my Master's Certificate there was little use in my looking for a master's berth for I had not yet sailed as first mate. To put this right, I served for about two years as first mate in some of the old wooden ships that were trading between Canada and Maryport with timber. This was a hard life, but good training for a young man.

I then got my first command—the brig *Bowes*, owned by Messrs Ritson of Maryport.

9

The *Bowes*

In his Memoirs, William has very little to say about this stage of his career, but from three of the brig *Bowes*' Official Logbooks—discovered among the papers of the late Dr Crerar, the Maryport historian—we glimpse some of the day-to-day incidents that occurred during this first command. They would have been familiar to most sea captains of the time—and in essence, no doubt, to most sea captains of today.

> Brig *Bowes*. 6 am May 6th 1872. Palma. John Black A.B. refusing to commence work, to discharge cargo, as ordered by the ship's officers. Engaged a man from shore as a substitute at daily wages charged against the said seaman. At 7 am asked him to give a reason for refusing duty. He said the only reason for doing so was one or more of the seamen suspected him of stealing, he wished to see the British Consul. 10 am still refusing to work, and requesting to go to the Consul. I gave him leave to do so, with orders to return to the ship immediately he had seen the Consul. At 3 pm returned on board in a state of intoxication and commenced annoying the people on board.
>
> William A. Nelson.
James Peters, Mate.

> In consideration of J. Black's general good conduct during remainder of voyage, no Penalty imposed.
>
> William A. Nelson.
5/7/72
James Peters.

May 6th 1872. Palma. John McKearly A.B. off duty complaining of being ill with the Piles. Treatment, one teaspoonful of Sulphur in a glass of water, and soothing lotion for a wash, as per 'Medical Guide'.

May 10th. Returned to Duty.

March 10th 1873. Palma. Whereas Thomas Stamper engaged as Cook & Steward, being totally unfit to fulfil his duties and being dirty and unclean in his habits and about his work, I have requested H.M. Consul at this port that I might be allowed to discharge him, which request cannot be granted at this Port. I hereby disrate him from being cook from this date and reduce his wages from £4 per month to £3 per month.

March 11th, 8 pm. Read this statement over to Thomas Stamper and asked him what reply he had to make to it. He said he had no reply to make.

Swansea. March 29th 1874. Articles signed this day. April 1st, Mate and Cook & Steward on duty. April 2nd, John Johnston & Thomas Steward A.B.s on duty. April 4th, H. Greavy, Boatswain, and Charles Dean commenced work this day.

April 6th 1874. Ship ready for sea, with the exception of part of the crew not being on board. At 5 am commenced to unmoor the ship and hauled down to the Dock Gates. John Angus, Mate, Henry Greavy, Boatswain and Michael Fegan, Cook & Steward, John Johnston and Thomas Stewart A.B.s being on duty at the time. After the vessel was hauled to the Dock Gates, John Johnston and Thomas Stewart went on shore without leave. At 7 am John W. Tucker A.B. came on board. 7.30 am being then near high water, and the vessel being in the way of other vessels proceeding to sea, had to tow out to sea. After towing to the Mumble Roads, had to leave the vessel in charge of the Pilot and called a shore boat, then passing, to take me on shore to look for the remainder of the crew, who had signed to be on board at 8 am on the 4th. At 11.30 am having with much difficulty got the remainder of the crew (consisting of the following: John Johnston A.B. Thomas Stewart A.B. David Griffiths A.B. Thomas Davies O.S. and Charles Dean O.S.) collected together, had to engage a Boat to take the men and their clothes on board. Returned on board at Noon and the crew turned to their duty. The following expenses, having been paid on account of the above, will be deducted from those of the crew on whose account the money was paid, from each one an equal amount. Expenses paid on account of the above.

To Boat to take Master on shore to look for the crew	—: 2:0
Boat to bring the men and their clothes on board	1:10:0
Extra Pilotage. Pilot being left in charge while the Master was on shore looking for the crew.	11:6
Total	£2: 3:6

The above statement having been read over to the several parties mentioned, and on being asked if they had any reply to make, they said it was quite right.

W. A. Nelson, Master.

Monday the 13th day of April, 1874. Latitude 49°: 34′ North, Longtitude 11°: 24′ West. At 11.45 am ship hove-to on the starboard tack, wind N.W. blowing a very heavy gale and a fearful sea running. Ship having two close-reefed topsails set. A fearful sea broke on board, which unfortunately washed the Mate John Angus overboard, we being unable to render him any assistance on account of the fearful storm blowing at the time, and the condition the ship was in after the sea had swept over her. The same sea swept away three men from the pumps, but they fortunately held on by the lee main rigging. I was in the cabin at the time the sea struck the ship. When I got up on deck I found the Long Boat broke up into pieces. The Jolly Boat landed on the lee rail, but before we could get the tackles hooked on, the ship gave a lurch to leeward and the Boat went overboard and filled directly. At the same time the Galley, Light-screens, Bulwarks from the port side were swept away. The after-hatch and cabin skylight were stove in, also the afterhouse and companion were started. The Binnacle and all cooking utensils all swept away at the same time. At 4 a.m. on Tuesday the 14th, wore ship and steered for the Channel again to repair damage.

Signed Wednesday the 15th day of April, 1874.

> William A. Nelson, Master
> Michael Fegan, Cook & Steward
> Henry Greavy, Boatswain.

After making several voyages to Spain, returning to Maryport with iron ore for the blast furnaces there, William and the brig *Bowes* concentrated mainly on the Canadian timber trade. This experience was to stand him in good stead when he went into partnership with his elder brother Jonathan in the ship *New Brunswick*. Just prior to the purchase of this vessel, from the 5th October, 1879 to 30th July, 1880, William made one voyage from Cardiff to Callao in command of the famous little barque *Mary Moore*, a vessel he was to sail with great success some seven years later.

Meanwhile, on 8th January, 1876, William had married Jane Scott, daughter of James Scott, Blacksmith, in the Parish Church at Birkenhead. Twin sons were born on 5th October, 1876. One, christened Benjamin, died on 10th May, 1877. The other was probably stillborn, as he is not named in the family Bible. Margaret Thorburn, named after Jane's mother, was born on 15th February, 1879, but died soon afterwards. Surviving children were: Mary Ellen, born 6th March, 1883; James, born 15th December, 1885; Margaret, born 23rd November, 1887; Jane and Isabella (twins) born 23rd March, 1890.

The children were sent to Quaker boarding schools after starting in Maryport. The girls, who were encouraged by their father to train for careers, went to Brookfield School at Wigton. James was sent to the Quaker school at Penketh near Warrington, because (like so many mothers of those days) Jane Nelson hoped that sending him inland would make him forget about making the sea his career. It didn't. Indeed, his schoolmaster fostered James's nautical interest—for which, as we enjoy his beautiful ship paintings, we may be truly thankful.

It was during the 1870s and 1880s, while William Nelson was gaining experience as a sailing ship commander in such maritime 'cart-horses' as the brig *Bowes* and the *New Brunswick*, that the clipper ship era came to an end. It was never his destiny to command such a vessel. A pity, in a way.

Today, the term 'clipper' is inclined to be loosely used, but its true meaning is precise. A clipper was any cargo-carrying vessel—of any size and of any rig—that was designed to sail as fast as possible. This meant that with the fine lines necessary for speed, cargo space was sacrificed. Compared with the total number of commercial sailing vessels, very few clippers were ever built and they were at their peak for a very short time—from about 1845 to 1870.

Some of the most famous clippers were those beautiful vessels turned out by the British and American ship-building yards during the 1850s and '60s: *Lightning, Cairngorm, Stornoway, Crest of the Wave, City of Nankin, James Baines, Champion of the Seas, Cutty Sark, Taeping, Ariel, Serica, Sir Lancelot, Thermopylae* and others, designed for specific trades. But their days were numbered almost as they were being launched, for in the late 1860s the steamer was beginning to compete successfully with sail. By 1875 the day of the clipper was done.

The big full-lined iron or steel sailing ship cargo-carriers of the 1880s and 1890s—three- and four-masted barques and full-rigged ships of 1,500 and 2,500 tons, the 'windjammers' as they came to be known, were able to carry several times the amount of cargo of the small wooden ships of the '60s, and with a smaller crew in proportion to their tonnage. The *Ocean Queen*, a full-rigged ship of 630 tons sailing from Bristol to Quebec in 1855, had a total crew of 20. The *A. J. Fuller*, a full-rigger of nearly 2,000 tons on passage in the late 1890s, had a crew of 21. The big steel cargo-carrier of the 1890s could offer a reasonable return on investment even in the face of the steamer's triple expansion engine; but by the early 1900s the balance was firmly and permanently shifted in favour of steam.

Sailing his full-lined 2,000-ton *Auchencairn* and 1,800-ton *Acamas* with exceptional flair, William Nelson made passages in the 1890s and early 1900s that challenged those of the steamers as well as many potentially faster sailing ships. What he might have achieved in fast passages had he ever commanded one of those extreme clippers of the 1860s is a matter of conjecture. But one may safely assume that his times would have borne comparison with any ever logged.

IO

The *New Brunswick*

About 1880, my elder brother, Jonathan, and I, purchased the wooden barque *New Brunswick* from Messrs Andrew and Fraser of London. We were the largest shareholders. She was registered in my brother's name and it was arranged that I went in command.

We were fortunate in having one or two farmer friends who supplied sufficient prime Cumberland hams, potatoes and vegetables for the voyages to Canada and back, as these kept well in the colder Northern climate.

Interesting about those hams. A ham similar to William's, cured in the same place and in just the same way, hangs from a ceiling hook in my cottage as I write. It came from the nearby Cumbrian village of Waberthwaite, grown and cured on the same land by the farmers whose grandparents cured the hams William Nelson stocked his ships with a hundred years ago.

In those days, Waberthwaite hams were supplied to The White Star Line of Liverpool. The shipowner Thomas Henry Ismay, founder of The White Star, was in partnership with one of William's relatives, Philip Nelson. Both were Maryport men and knew a good ham when they tasted one. So did William Nelson know. And so do I!

To have sailed the same Solway waters and shared the same tastes gives me a pleasant feeling of affinity with this Cumbrian seaman I so greatly admire.

The *New Brunswick* was a fairly big ship, but she was getting old and scarcely suitable for any other trade except the timber business, so we employed her on the North Atlantic—bringing timber home mostly to Maryport or Ardrossan. This proved successful and we did very well.

Mrs Nelson made a voyage or two with me to Quebec during the summer months. But not really being very fond of the sea, she was more content to remain at home. Crossing the Atlantic in such a vessel is no joy ride at any time!

Looking back on it, it was just as well that my wife decided to stay at home. After seven years of regular trading across the North Atlantic the old ship, now seventeen years old, found the strain too much for her and foundered during a heavy gale. At least, she became so water-logged that we had to abandon her.

We were rescued by another ship, and I returned home in the White Star liner *Teutonic*. This would be in 1887.

That ended my career in the Canadian timber trade, and I was soon to be sailing a better ship much farther afield. But I maintain that, ailing as she was, the *New Brunswick* served us well, taking into account the dangers associated with the trade such as fogs, icebergs, heavy gales and blizzards. It must be remembered that there were no radio beacons then, and the few lighthouses that did exist could not be compared to those of today.

My next command was the barque *Mary Moore*.

II

The *Mary Moore*

The *Mary Moore* was a composite vessel (that is with iron frames planked with wood). She was a trim, handy craft, strongly built but with fine lines and her main skysail yard gave her a pleasing appearance. The hull was black, except for the metal sheathing; the masts and spars painted white. She was originally built for the China tea trade and her sailing qualities were very good. With only a moderate breeze she did a comfortable 9 knots 'by the wind', and 13 knots in a fair wind. As she was also good at beating to windward we were rarely passed by any other vessel.

How easy this is to understand. This was the opportunity William had dreamed about while stitching canvas on the *James Jardine* and, latterly, the *Sevilla* and watching bunglers wasting good sailing chances. The *Mary Moore*

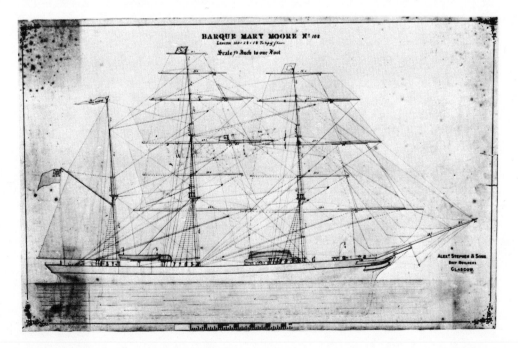

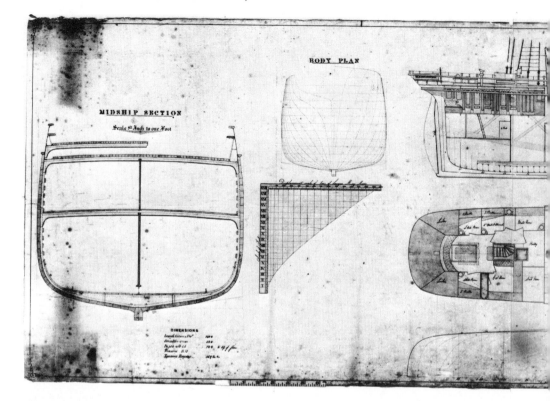

was not a true clipper, but she was fast and came nearer to being a clipper than any other ship he was ever to command. At the time he knew simply that she was 'handy' and that here was a chance to give a taste of his quality.

> In the *Mary Moore* I made very regular passages to and from the West Coast of South America. The shortest passage was 78 days, and the longest 88 days.

For a little 500-tonner this was splendidly consistent sailing. On every voyage to the South American coast she took the east/west passage round Cape Horn in her stride. Occasional round voyages to Australia were treated almost as holidays—except, perhaps, for the problems of charter . . .

> Major Norman, the *Mary Moore*'s owner, evidently had faith in my business efficiency and integrity, for after the ship left England on a voyage he never bothered to write to me and give me his ideas on subsequent charters. Yet on occasions I would have been glad of his views, for chartering could be a very worrying proposition. I remember once when we were loading a general cargo in London for Adelaide, Major Norman came on board to see me. Before he

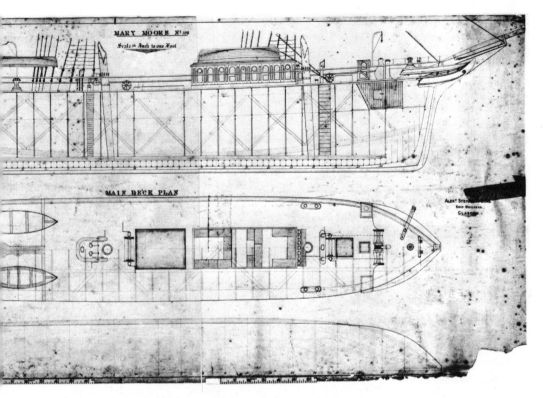

left, I asked him to write to me on the voyage and give me instructions. He replied: 'Take the ship away. Imagine she is yours. I feel confident you will do the best possible in my interests.'

So off I went, and thought no more about this conversation until at Adelaide, to my surprise, I received a letter of instruction—the first I had ever had. Ironically, it arrived too late to be complied with. I had made a fast passage out, and while the cargo was discharging had arranged a charter to load for London with wool, tallow and what was probably one of the first consignments of tinned rabbit. The ship was nearly loaded when Major Norman's letter arrived instructing me to 'proceed in ballast to Newcastle NSW and there purchase on the Owner's account a cargo of coal (about 1,000 tons) then proceed to the West Coast and sell it there.'

Well—at that stage there was nothing I could do about it. And just as well as things turned out, for it transpired that some vessels *did* take cargoes in this way, and most of them showed a loss owing to a falling market and long delays on the coast!

We made a good run home and the ship turned over a nice profit for the owner. He was so pleased that he gave me a handsome bonus.

Just before leaving London a package had come on board requiring 'careful and special stowage'. For safety I placed it in my cabin. On my arrival at

Adelaide, the Governor of South Australia came in person to claim this mysterious package. When I showed him where it was stowed he asked me whether I had entertained myself on the voyage 'to some nice music?' When I shook my head he smiled and told me I should have opened it up, as it contained the latest instrument in home entertainment—a musical box! It must have been the first to arrive in Australia.

William would have enjoyed that musical box. As his grandchildren remember, he had a great love of music—without, they think, having much musical knowledge. Certainly, under that rugged exterior, there was something of a sentimentalist. One of his favourite pieces, which he played on his early wax-cylinder gramophone, was Leonora's aria in *Il Trovatore*—until someone who understood Italian told him it was the song of 'a soul in agony'; then he wouldn't listen to it again.

On the West Coast voyages Mr Hugh Jones was my first mate. He was a fine gentleman and seaman. We and our families formed a life-long friendship. He later left 'sail' and for many years commanded tramp steamers sailing out of Hartlepool and Cardiff.

On one of my West Coast voyages Mrs Nelson accompanied me. But Cape Horn and the sea in general never appealed to her much. On future occasions she preferred to join the ship at Falmouth or Queenstown.

Major Norman the owner was related to Mr Ritson of Maryport, and in 1888 I left the *Mary Moore* to go in command of one of Messrs Ritsons' barques, the *William Ritson*.

The barque *Mary Moore* (618 12/94 tons o.m.) was built in Glasgow in 1867/8 by Alexander Stephen & Sons. She was to be a composite barque classed 15AI @ Lloyds and to cost £17.95 per ton register. Building took eighteen months, yielding a builder's profit of £705 with £277 allocated for yard rent and overheads.

12

The *William Ritson*

Abstracts from log of barque 'William Ritson'; Capt. W. A. Nelson		
Date	**Garston to Iquique**	**Days out**
1888		
June 13th	Left Garston, coal cargo, Cast off tug Pt. Lynus	
June 16th	*Departure* from Old Head of Kinsale	
June 30th	Sighted Palma Island	14
July 3rd	Signalled ship 'Giovanni' of Aberdeen, Newport to Cape Blanco 21 days out	17
July 12th	J. Foley, AB, fell from aloft and broke his arm	
July 16th	Transferred Foley to a French Steamer	
July 18th	Signalled 4-masted ship 'Nile' 34 days out from Cardiff	32
July 19th	Crossed Equator in Long. 27 West	33
Aug. 23rd	Of Cape Horn, strong westerly gale, snow & hail	68
Sept. 19th	*Arrived Iquique*, passage from departure	95
	From Iquique ship proceeded to Carrizal to load.	

	Carrizal to Channel for Orders	
1889		
Jan. 22nd	Sailed from Carrizal	
Feb. 13th	Passed Cape Horn	22
March 7th	Signalled ship 'W Q H K' from San Francisco to Fleetwood, 75 days out	
March 17th	Signalled barque 'Rokeby Hall' London to Newcastle, N.S.W.	
March 18th	Crossed Equator in Long. 29 West	55
April 3rd	Signalled ship 'J D R B' Sydney to London 88 days out	
April 4th	Signalled ship 'Romanoff' Geelong to London 95 days out. Six vessels in sight.	
April 8th	Signalled vessel 'H D G F' Frisco to Hull, 100 days out.	
April 21st	*Arrived Queenstown*, passage from Carrizal	89

In 1888 I took over command of the barque *William Ritson* at Garston where a cargo of coal was loaded. We sailed on June 13 for Iquique.

We were held up off the 'Horn' for a while with the usual westerly gales and made the passage in 95 days, the ship having no turn of speed.

From Iquique we proceeded to Carrizal and loaded for home. We made the passage to Queenstown in 89 days, arriving April 1889.

After making the one voyage in this ship I was appointed to a larger vessel of the same company: the *Rising Star*.

William Nelson's typically laconic account glides smoothly over the mind, to be as quickly forgotten—unless we stop to think about it, and to read between the lines. 'Held up off the "Horn" . . . Westerly gales . . . No turn of speed . . .' These are the ingredients of an interminable voyage. And yet, in a vessel as slow as the *William Ritson*, our man makes passages of 95 days out and 89 days back, and in perfect safety.

Bigger ships frequently took longer than that to sail round Cape Horn and back. Many failed to get round at all. Most masters of faster ships would have been happy with William's times. Certainly, his employers were.

Maryport was famous for its fine seamen, but Messrs Ritsons the owners of the *William Ritson* knew by now that—even by Maryport's high standards—in this ex-apprentice from their sail-loft they had an outstanding ship's master. As well as being builders they were shrewd businessmen. They were not in shipping to make a reputation at the expense of profits. The ships they built and controlled were excellent vessels, but they were not designed as clippers for a specialized trade, such as tea or fruit, where speed was paramount. They were full-lined, long-haul 'work-horses', for carrying cargoes of coal, grain, nitrate, cement, timber, rails. Fast passages were a welcome bonus.

Safety plus speed spelled profit. William Nelson was safe and he was fast. So—give him command of the *Rising Star*, a bigger ship. It made good sense.

The barque *Rising Star* had been built twelve years earlier by Birrell Stenhouse at Dumbarton on the Clyde. Ritsons had just bought her from her Maryport owner, Captain Melmore. She had done nothing spectacular. She was no clipper; potentially, not much faster than the *William Ritson*. But she was bigger. She could carry more cargo. In Captain Nelson's hands she would make a safe passage. She might even make a smart one. So—transfer him from the *William Ritson*, sell him some shares in the *Rising Star* and let them see what he could do.

13

The *Rising Star*

Abstracts from log of barque 'Rising Star'; Capt. W. A. Nelson

Date	Antwerp to Valparaiso	Days out
1889		
Nov. 30th	Left Flushing in tow, cast off tug same day	
Dec. 1st	*Took departure* from St Catherine's Point	
Dec. 8th	Passed Madeira Island	7
Dec. 13th	Sighted Cape St Antonio, Cape Verde Islands	12
Dec. 24th	Crossed Equator in long. 28 West	23
Dec. 28th	Passed 2 barques and 1 ship going same way	
1890		
Jan. 4th	Spoke barque 'Per Adua'	
Jan. 11th	Parted company with barque 'Per Adua'	
Jan. 13th	Sighted land near Cape Corrientis	
Jan. 22nd	Passed through straits of Le Maire	52
Jan. 24th	Off Cape Horn, spoke barque 'Glamis' from London to San Diego 50 Days out	54
Feb. 5th	*Arrived Valparaiso* passage from departure From Valparaiso proceeded to Iquique to load	66

The *Rising Star* was an iron vessel, the first I had ever sailed, all my previous ships having been of wood or of composite construction in which pumping was almost a daily necessity. This ship, in which I had bought a number of shares, was strongly-built and with rather full lines, which made her decidedly slow even under the most favourable conditions. In fact, her speed rarely exceeded 9 knots. And yet, as fate decreed, she sailed the fastest passage I ever made out to the American West Coast.

On the 30th November 1889 we sailed from Antwerp with a general cargo for Valparaiso.

Passed Cape Verde Isles 12 days out.

Crossed the Equator 23 days out.

Cape Horn 54 days out.

Arrived at Valparaiso 66 days out from St Catherine's Pt. (Departure), or 67 days port to port.

Only on one occasion did our daily run attain 240 miles, about 10 knots. But we kept up a steady daily average of some 180 miles.

From Valparaiso we proceeded to Iquique and there loaded for home. The passage to Falmouth was made in 93 days; thus completing the round voyage, in eight months, out of which three months were spent on the coast.

This really was astonishing. How did he drive this run-of-the-mill cargo-carrier half way round the world, taking on Cape Horn as he went, in 66 days? An amalgam, one supposes, of razor-edged seamanship, accurate navigation and sheer strength of character. The last, perhaps, most important of all. Long afterwards, in conversation, he said of this passage: 'The ship wasn't particularly fast, but she hated to stop—so I just kept her going!'

Date	Iquique to Channel for orders	Days out
1890		
May 3rd	Sailed from Iquique, light baffling winds for 7 days	
May 30th	Off Cape Horn, strong S.W. wind heavy squalls	27
June 28th	Crossed Equator in long. 28 West	56
July 1st	Spoke barque 'Antilles' from Liverpool to Conception 27 days out	
July 8th	Passed several vessels	
Aug. 3rd	Sighted Bishop Rock, Scillies	92
August 4th	*Arrived Falmouth*, passage port to port	93

Date	Tyne to Valparaiso	Days out
1890		
Sept. 24th	Sailed from Tyne, cast off tug same day	
Sept. 29th	Passed Isle of Wight	
Oct. 3rd	*Took departure* from Scilly Isles	

Auchencairn, built at Maryport in 1891, painted by the Australian painter and photographer Godfrey.

Mary Moore in 1888 during William Nelson's command, by an unknown artist.

Acamas painted by James Nelson.

Paddle-tug *Florence* towing the barque *Grimello* into Maryport during the gale of 18th October, 1883.
Painting by William Mitchell of Maryport.

Oct. 30th	Becalmed off Cape Verde Isles	27
Nov. 13th	Crossed Equator in Long. 29 West	41
Nov. 14th	Spoke ship 'Corialanus' of London, from London to Brisbane, 42 days out	42
Nov. 23rd	Spoke ship 'Maraval' of Glasgow from London to San Diego 52 days out	51
Nov. 27th	Spoke barque 'Alice Platt' from Ucivara to Iquique 37 days out	55
Dec. 17th	Passed through Straits of Le Maire. 2 ships, 1 barque	
Dec. 18th	Off Cape Horn, fresh S.S.W. gale and rain in company of squalls	76
1891		
Jan. 5th	*Arrived Valparaiso*, passage from departure	94
	Ship proceeded to Iquique to load	

Date	Iquique to Channel for orders	Days out
1891		
April 25th	Sailed from Iquique	
May 11th	Spoke ship 'Drumeltan'	
May 22nd	Passed Cape Horn, strong S.W. gale, squally and clear	27
June 6th	Spoke ship 'Drumlarig', from Astoria to Cork	
June 19th	Crossed Equator in long. 28½ West	55
June 22nd	Spoke ship 'Rottingham' of London, from Melbourne to Queenstown, 69 days out	58
June 25th	Spoke ship 'Garsdale' steering south, 26 days out. All well	
July 14th	Spoke ship 'Agnes Oswald' from Melbourne to Falmouth, 98 days out	
July 27th	Spoke ship 'Lismore' from New Zealand to Falmouth, 100 days out	
July 29th	Spoke two vessels in company, both are 41 days from the Equator, no better luck than ourselves	40
Aug. 10th	*Arrived Falmouth*, passage port to port	107

I only made one more voyage in the *Rising Star*, and our times to and from the West Coast were not nearly so good, being 94 days outwards and 107 days homeward. This was the first time in my career so far that I had failed to do the passage in either direction in less than 100 days.

It is characteristic of William that he offers no excuses for what, for him, were slow passages (although other ships at the time made passages that were no better, if as good). A glance at the weather as recorded in the various logs shows periods of extended calm. But he had already done enough to show his true worth. And now he was to be offered command of a new ship—one that despite initial set-backs was quick to make a name.

After leaving the *Rising Star* I took command of a new four-masted barque the owners were building—the *Auchencairn*.

Note: The *Rising Star* was another lucky ship that had a long and varied career. After I left her she was sold and I got all my money back that I invested in her. At some time or another she was sold to the Italians and renamed 'Solicito'. Again in 1908 she was sold to the French and renamed 'Marius Ricoux'; later she again came under the British flag and finally sold for service as a coal hulk in Sydney N.S.W. (Lloyds reported her still afloat as a hulk in 1939.)

14

The *Auchencairn*

The steel four-masted barque *Auchencairn* was named after a village on the Scottish side of the Solway Firth, where friends of Mr Ritson owned a large estate.

Mr George Monkhouse, a master-rigger of great repute in West Cumberland ports, was responsible for the masting and rigging. This was carried out in the wet-dock; a small locomotive being used for lifting the masts and yards into position.

The vessel had fine lines, and a big sheer which tended to make her wet in the waist when running in heavy weather. She was also inclined to be somewhat crank. Although she had a good turn of speed and could do 13 knots, I never got the winds in the Atlantic that would have enabled me to equal the times of the *Mary Moore* between the Channel and the Equator; or, to be more correct, between the Channel and Cape Horn. Nevertheless, we made some good passages.

VOYAGE I

In October, 1891 we left Maryport for Cardiff, with 500 tons of ballast, in tow of the Clyde tug *Flying Eagle*. To have proceeded under sail we should have required about 1,000 tons.

As we were passing out of the piers, the Harbour Master (my younger brother, Captain Benjamin Nelson) informed me that he had just received a wire to hoist the South Cone, as a strong Southerly gale was expected. But since the weather was fine I decided to carry on, thinking that if necessary I could put into Ransey Bay or Holyhead for shelter.

We had got nearly as far as Holyhead when the wind increased to a whole gale from the S.E. There was no chance of our finding shelter. The tug could make no headway against the wind, but gamely hung-on broad out on our bow, for in spite of our having a storm-spanker and jigger-staysail set, the ship kept falling off until the wind was almost abeam.

The gale increased in fury as the night wore on. Our main anxiety was whether the towing hawser would part, or whether the tug skipper would slip the rope and seek his own safety. However, the tug nursed the ship very nicely and we finally brought up in Kingstown Roads. There we rode the gale with both anchors out.

The gale was severely felt at Maryport, we heard later. Many houses having slates and even roofs blown off.

The crew of the *Auchencairn* being mainly local, Mrs Nelson had many callers seeking news of the ship, which they feared might have foundered. There was no radio in those days, of course, and she could only remind them that 'No news is good news.' In fact, several days elapsed before they heard that the ship was safe at Kingstown.

The weather continued stormy and we were delayed about ten days before we sailed again. At last, however, we arrived safely at Cardiff, and I understand the tug skipper received a purse of money from the underwriters for his 'meritorious conduct'.

At Cardiff was the now famous ship *Grace Harwar*, commanded by my friend Captain Sewell of Maryport. She was almost new, then, and I fancy belonged to Messrs Montgomery of London. She looked very well with her freshly-painted sides of black ports, or squares, on a white band. Captain Sewell died at Frisco soon afterwards.

The *Grace Harwar* while under the Red Ensign was commanded by Cumberland men for many years, including Captains Briscoe and Fearon.

Fearon, like the Nelsons, Dixon, Messenger, Hodgson, Rich, Briscoe, Collins and many other fine windjammer captains, was a Maryport man. A resolute leader and man of courage, he was another of those sensible ship's masters who cared for their crews. 'Feed the men well,' he advised. 'With plenty of hot coffee at night-time; and a good stove with plenty of coal in the fo'c'sle and half-deck.' In turn, his men respected him. And on a howling night in 1891 off Cape Horn when in command of the *Dawpool*, he reaped the benefit.

With the ship running before a gale, tremendous seas stove-in the main hatch. Two attempts to secure it ended in failure, the men being repeatedly swept by incoming waves the length of the maindeck. Panic stricken, knowing that the ship was likely to founder at any moment, the crew lost their nerve and stayed where there were, huddled in a group. Fighting his way forward along the flooded deck, with seas sweeping aboard and sluicing down into the main hold, Fearon found his crew cowering under the fo'c'sle head. Desperately, he urged them to 'Come out and fight like men, not die like rats'; adding that he would do the job himself, if they would help him.

Inspired by this man whom they had always respected, a few struggled aft with him to the ruins of the main hatch . . . and the others followed. Just in time, they succeeded in securing the hatchway with a spare sail—after which, the ship was brought safely to the wind.

Captain Guy de Mattos, then an apprentice on the *Dawpool*, wrote later: 'A truly terrible night, one not easily forgotten. Captain Fearon behaved with remarkable coolness.' That night, he said, was the worst at sea he ever experienced.

Apart from crew panic and loss of nerve—which all but lost the old *James Jardine* and nearly finished off the *Dawpool*, there were so many ways of losing a windjammer. The *Auchencairn* might have been wrecked on her maiden voyage before a sail was set. That first night in the Irish Sea, towing south from Maryport, must have been a close-run thing.

In his Memoirs, William treats it calmly enough; but I sense the apprehension. He had sailed in the face of his brother's gale warning, and for hour after hour hung almost helpless on the end of a tow-rope. Underwriters were not noted for their generosity in throwing purses of money about. The skipper of the tug *Flying Eagle* was a brave man. How easy to have slipped his cable in the darkness and run for safety. But he didn't. I can imagine him out there in the blackness on the *Auchencairn*'s weather bow crouched behind his salt-streaked 'dodger', heading the *Flying Eagle* into the teeth of the storm, the tug's smoke-stack belching sparks and soot, her bows butting into steepening seas with waves sluicing green across her well-deck, spray pluming up over her nose like gunsmoke. He deserved his 'purse'.

As the record of that great gale relates, Maryport's fears for the safety of the *Auchencairn* were well founded.

> Great damage was done to shipping [reported *The West Cumberland Times* of Wednesday, October 21st, 1891]. In the Irish Channel the storm raged fiercely, and the mail steamer *Connaught* had a very rough passage, drifting helplessly for some time with her paddle arm broken, and arriving five hours late at Holyhead. The high tide, lashed by the strong wind, caused much damage in the Isle of Man. At Douglas, great waves swept the promenade, ripping the roadway, displacing the tram lines, flooding many of the houses . . . A long stretch of the Furness Railway near Arnside was damaged, and traffic stopped; and the Great Western Railway suffered a serious landslip. In Nottinghamshire, Lincolnshire, and some of the southern counties, rivers overflowed and the floods spread over many acres.

Fire at sea, storms, icebergs, collision, dismasting, shifting cargoes, uncharted rocks, recklessness, drunkenness, bad landfalls—they could all lose ships. And did, with alarming frequency. But there was another hazard, insidious in its danger for all too often it came unnoticed: fatigue. The loss of the fine Maryport barque *Brier Holme* seems to have been due to a navigational error almost certainly caused by exhaustion. There must have been many similar cases.

Commanded by that popular and highly experienced Maryport master, Captain John Rich, the *Brier Holme* was wrecked in a gale off the West Coast of Tasmania. Her fate was unknown until the sole survivor, Oscar Larson, a Norwegian, was found living rough in the bush, subsisting from tinned food salvaged from the wreck. According to his statement, on the night of November 5th, 1904, after a long spell of terrible weather, the *Brier Holme* was hove-to under close topsails. The night was dark. Just before midnight, during the mate's watch on deck, the vessel was driven on rocks at Elliott's Cove. The impact caused the dynamite, which formed a large portion of the cargo, to explode, and Larsen thought that the captain and some of the crew were blown up ... 'The sea was terrific ... and the breakers quickly completed the destruction on deck . . .'

Just prior to that fateful voyage, Captain Rich had written in reply to a letter from his son:

> I am very sorry to hear of the stranding of the 'Manchester Trader' on the island of Auticosti, Gulf of St Lawrence. I knew the ship well and have often been in the vicinity of this island, rather too close sometimes, when I was in the Quebec Trade as 1st and 2nd officer, and the time I was sweethearting dear Mother. *Oh dear those were happy days,* when we could walk 10 miles or more and never feel tired, but now a few yards satisfies a fellow . . .

When she struck the reef in the darkness of that dreadful November night, the *Brier Holme* was sailing on dead-reckoning. There seems to have been a position error. Captain Rich was below at the time, exhausted. It was his last voyage before retirement . . .

William Nelson escaped a similar fate—but perhaps only just. His return to sea for 'one more voyage' after retirement could easily have ended in disaster when, with his first mate insane and second mate uncertificated, he found himself in mid-ocean with no other competent watchkeeper. But that was in 1907. In 1891 he was approaching the peak of his career. Even so, his fine maiden passage in the *Auchencairn* was to end in sad anti-climax.

> The *Auchencairn* left Cardiff on the 24th November,1891 for San Francisco. We made a good run to the Horn and there met with exceptionally heavy gales.
> F. Watkins, ordinary seaman, fell from the main topgallant yard and was lost overboard.

Hit by heavy seas the ship started a leak. This became so persistent that, during the ten days of bad weather, steam was raised on the donkey boiler operating the pumps.

When fine weather eventually came, the leak stopped as mysteriously as it had started.

On 21st March, 1892 we reached Frisco. Storms notwithstanding, we had made a fairly good passage of 118 days; but arrived only to find a great many ships laid-up waiting for lucrative freights.

After the cargo was discharged we, also, joined the great fleet of idle shipping—and stayed 'put' for nearly eighteen months!

Abstracts from log of four-masted barque 'Auchencairn'; Capt W. A. Nelson

Date	Cardiff to San Francisco	Days out
1891		
Nov. 24th	Left Cardiff, coal cargo, cast off tug at Lundy, *Departure*	
Dec. 13th	Passed Cape St Antonio, Cape Verde Isles	19
Dec. 21st	Crossed Equator in Long. 27 West	27
Dec. 22nd	Spoke barque 'Prince Rupert' from Cardiff to Rio Janeiro 33 days out	28
Dec. 23rd	Spoke a Schooner Yacht from Sydney CB, to British Columbia, 26 days out	29
1892		
Jan. 14th	Exchanged longitudes with S.S. 'Gulf of Guinea'	
Jan. 23rd	Off Cape Horn, during a gale F. Watkins fell from main topgallant yard and was lost overboard	62
Feb. 13th	Fore and aft schooner in company	
Feb. 26th	Crossed Equator (Pacific) in long. 114 West	94
March 21st	*Arrived San Francisco*, passage port to port Owing to low freights ship laid up about 18 months	118

It must have been depressing in the extreme for William to arrive in port after making a reasonable passage in his fine new ship, only to find the harbour full of laid-up vessels, and himself condemned to idleness—a frustrating period of long inactivity.

But by now the writing was on the wall for the windjammer. With a crew of half the size and the capacity to take double the load and do its work faster, spending less time in port loading and discharging, the steamer's advantages were beginning to tell. With reductions in crew and penny-pinching in stores and gear a big sailing vessel could still take a cargo half-way round the world at low cost. And for a time the larger ships fought back with donkey boilers and winches that speeded up the work in port. But the end was already in sight.

> Steamers can now be built at less cost than sailing ships [said the *Shipping Gazette and Lloyds List Weekly Summary*]. The great size of the modern tramp, with its economic consumption of coal and its enormous bunker capacity, renders it the most formidable competitor even where formerly it hardly dared show its black sides and ungainly form.

Until the 1860s, steamships posed no threat to sail for long ocean passages. Their coal consumption, with the low boiler steam pressures and simple engines of the time, was around 10 lb of coal per ton mile. They would, for example, have required around 140,000 tons of coal to take a 2,000-ton cargo from the United Kingdom to San Francisco. Thus, steam propulsion was used only on short-range duties such as were carried out by tugs or ferries, where speed, or freedom from dependence on wind direction, was all-important.

Between the 1850s and 1870s, however, developments in the quality of iron and boiler-making techniques allowed steam pressures to increase to 60lb per square inch, and 'improved compound-engines' to be introduced. This reduced coal consumption to about 1 lb per ton mile.

Over this period, too, sailing ships were being developed to their greatest efficiency as long-distance carriers, and for a time a balance between sail and steam was achieved. Indeed, even after the opening of the Suez Canal in 1869, which benefited steam ships, most of the freight to and from the East Indies, Australia and the West Coast of South America was still being carried by sailing ships. But in the 1890s the introduction of stronger steel for boilers, allowing steam pressures to be increased to 200 lb per square inch, with triple-expansion steam engines, reduced fuel consumption to the almost unbelievably low figure of half-an-ounce per ton mile.

This improvement in coal consumption was so dramatic that, by the end of the last century, a first-class steamer could carry one ton of cargo one mile using heat in her furnace equivalent to that generated by burning one sheet of good quality Victorian writing paper!

Strangely, the man who did as much as any other to bring about this improvement in steamship performance—that great Liverpool engineer and ship-owner Alfred Holt—founded the shipping company which Captain Nelson's son and son-in-law joined after serving their time in sail.

It is true that sail enjoyed a short return to glory during the upheaval of the First World War. 1914–15 saw a sudden boost in the building of sailing vessels of all sizes. Indeed, those owners who built soon enough made huge profits. Old and decrepit ships, fitted out for sea again, made fortunes for their owners. Between 1916 and 1919 some 800 big sailing ships and an unknown number of smaller sailing vessels were launched. And once again the power of the wind came into its own. But it was short-lived. By 1920 the boom was over. The post-war shipyards met the demand for steam and motor tonnage much more rapidly than most people had thought possible. The new fleet of sail disappeared almost as quickly as it had materialized. In 1927, two years before William Nelson's death, the last big British square-rigger, the full-rigged ship *William Mitchell*, went to the breaker's yard.

But all this was in the future. In 1892, William was with the *Auchencairn*, anchored in San Francisco harbour.

There were worse places to be laid up during a shipping slump—as William recorded in his memoirs in 1905 when confined to the miseries of Pisagua—and he seems to have enjoyed himself well enough in San Francisco. But he was a seaman first and last and he fretted to be under sail again. Fortunately, the following year saw an improvement in freights. There were cargoes of grain to be carried, and thankfully William prepared the *Auchencairn* for sea.

Eventually we were again in commission and dry-docked for survey and cleaning. No trace of a leak could be found.

On the 22nd August, 1893 we sailed with a cargo of grain bound to the Channel for orders.

In Lat. 36 South and Long. 112 West, with the ship under lower topsails in a strong gale, two vivid flashes of lightning preceded a terrific squall. This threw the vessel nearly on her beam ends. The lee side of the deck was submerged and Able Seaman W. Stokes was washed overboard and drowned.

Steam was raised on the donkey boiler and the pumps worked continuously. The mystery leak had started again, and it was not until we got into the fine weather on the Atlantic side of the Horn that it stopped.

We crossed the Equator in the Atlantic 78 days out from Frisco and sighted Cape Clear 109 days out.

There we were forced to heave-to in a strong south-easterly gale, but arrived at Queenstown 111 days out.

Between Cape Horn and the Falkland Islands our progress had been delayed by the presence of numerous icebergs, two bergs in particular being several miles in length.

From Queenstown we were ordered to Stockton-on-Tees to discharge the grain, and there ended the *Auchencairn*'s maiden voyage.

Date	San Francisco to Channel for orders	Days out
1893		
Aug. 22nd	Left San Francisco, grain cargo, *Departure*	
Sept. 13th	Crossed Equator (Pacific), 114 West long.	22
Sept 28th	During very strong Southerly gale, ship under main lower topsail, lee rail submerged, W. Stokes AB. lost overboard	
Oct. 13th	Off Diego Ramarez Islands, spoke barque 'Godova' from Iquique to Falmouth 26 days out	52
Oct. 18th	Spoke American ship 'W. H. Macey' from Pisagua to New York, 36 days out	
Oct. 21st	Sighted two large ice-bergs to the N.E.	
Oct. 22nd	Sighted many more ice-bergs Lat. 46 S. Long. 41 West	
Nov. 8th	Crossed Equator (Atlantic) in 29½ West	78
Dec. 9th	Sighted Cape Clear, hove to in heavy Southerly gale	109
Dec. 11th	*Arrived Queenstown* passage port to port Ship proceeded to Stockton on Tees to discharge	111

Poor Able Seaman Stokes. Like Ordinary Seaman Watkins on the outward passage, he stood no chance of being rescued. To go overboard from a windjammer at sea, even in daylight, was to head for almost certain death. There were cases when some particularly fine piece of seamanship succeeded in fishing a seaman back on board again, but not many. Men could be lost three or four at a time if they were manning ropes when a big breaking sea washed out the main deck. The mate of the *Ancenis* was lucky. He went overboard with four seamen as the ship rolled into a big wave—but clung on to a rope and was swept back on deck with the next roll of the ship. Off the Horn, *seven* men were washed from the deck of the *Serena* when the ship was being hove-to in a worsening gale. Three of them held on to gear and were hauled back. Recording the loss of the others, the ship's log blamed: 'A squall of hurricane force and a mountainous sea . . .' For them, it was only a question of how long?

Usually, death came swiftly enough. Few shellbacks ever learnt to swim. If you went overboard, they said, it was better if you couldn't!

VOYAGE 2

Date	Tyne to Port Pirie, Australia	Days out
1894		
Feb. 14th	Left Tyne, cargo coal/coke	
Feb. 18th	Held up in Pentland Firth by strong Westerly gales	
Feb. 24th	Put into Long Hope for shelter	
March 8th	Sailed from Long Hope, via North Sea & Channel	
March 18th	Took *departure* from the Casquettes	
April 10th	Crossed Equator in Long. 23 West, 8 ships in company	23
April 21st	Sighted Martin Vaz Rocks. Spoke ship 'Glenlui'	34
April 24th	Lost sight of 'Glenlui' in rain squalls	
April 28th	Sighted Nightingale Island, & Tristan d'Achuna	41
May 7th	Crossed meridian of Cape Aghulas in Lat. 41 S.	50
June 12th	Arrived Port Pirie, passage from the Casquettes	86

From Stockton the old paddle tug *Victoria* towed us to the Tyne where the ship dry-docked. Again a special inspection was made to endeavour to find the mystery leak, which seemed to happen only in bad weather. Mr Ritson, the owner, travelled from Maryport to see the ship in dry-dock; but none of us, including two surveyors, could find any defects or leaky rivets. This was disappointing because a quantity of grain had been damaged by salt water.

We left the Tyne on the 14th February, 1894, and since there was a fresh southerly wind I decided to make the Pentland Firth passage by going North about.

We were nearly through when the wind suddenly shifted to the westward and a series of strong gales set in against us. What with a head wind and the tidal stream that ran so strongly to the eastward, we could do little or nothing. Eventually I put into Long Hope for shelter, and lay there waiting for better weather.

For day after day the wind continued to blow from the westward—so, on the 8th March I turned about and took the North Sea and Channel route. We took our departure from the Casquettes on the 18th March.

Twenty-three days later the Equator was crossed and we arrived at Port Pirie 86 days from the time of departure.

After the cargo was discharged I happened to notice a trickle of water coming from the butt of a plate in the run of the ship. On investigation it proved to be responsible for the mysterious leak that had worried us so often. The ship evidently 'worked' a lot under the counter in bad weather. The surveyor had extra transom beams fitted, and the plates re-riveted, which put an end to any further leaking.

From Port Pirie we sailed in ballast to Newcastle NSW, where a cargo of coal was loaded. Thence to San Francisco.

Riding out a heavy gale under lower topsails in Lat. 33 South and Long. 169 East, an exceptionally high sea heeled the ship over and shifted a quantity of cargo. While she lay with her lee rail under water, a fierce squall blew away two of the lower topsails. We were hove-to like this for three days, before the gale abated and the vessel could be trimmed upright.

In spite of this delay we made the passage to Frisco in 64 days.

Date	Newcastle N.S.W. to San Francisco	Days out
1894		
Aug. 29th	Left Newcastle, coal cargo. *Departure*	
Sept. 4th	In Lat. 33 S. Long. 169 E., ship under lower topsails when a heavy squall struck ship throwing her over until the lee side of deck was under water, coal cargo shifted at the same time, lost two lower topsails and fore topmast staysail. Strong Easterly gale continued 3 days, ship hove to	
Sept. 28th	Crossed Equator in long. 150½ West long.	30
Nov. 1st	*Arrived* San Francisco, passage port to port From Frisco ship proceeded to Portland, Oregon to load	64

Very significant that the *Auchencairn* should have her cargo shift after loading coal at Newcastle NSW. That fine windjammer master, James Learmont, who, like William Nelson, came from just north of the Solway, relates how he nearly lost his ship the *Bengairn* when bound for Valparaiso from Newcastle after loading coal. She was hit by a heavy squall in the Tasman Sea that knocked her on her beam ends—and the coal shifted.

'I thought I was getting a lesson on what happened to missing ships on that run, where so many had been lost', wrote Learmont later. 'So many, indeed, that underwriters were getting worried about the loss rate.'

Like most ships loading coal, the *Bengairn* was well down to her marks before being completely filled. This meant there was space left in her hold and that, unless the trimmers baffled it completely, the coal could shift. And although the usual 'shifting boards' were used, shift it did!

The *Bengairn*'s main hatch burst open. The sea flooded in. Somehow, just in time, the hatch was fothered with a sail. But Learmont and his crew knew it wouldn't last for long. The *Bengairn* was lying on her beam ends. To stop her from going right over they cut away the topgallant and royal masts and spars. Then they started to fight the coal. It took them five desperate days to retrim that cargo sufficiently for the ship to steer.

She still had a heavy list. But they saved her, even though her lee rail was underwater when, with a jury rig, she staggered into Sydney.

When Learmont got a quotation for re-rigging the *Bengairn*, the 'shore racketeers' bid more to do the job than the ship herself was worth. So— Learmont and his crew did it themselves. Referring to the shore-sharks, Lloyds said: 'Between them and fortune stood the experience of Captain Learmont and his regard for his owners' interests'. They praised him for 'his commendable resourcefulness, splendid audacity and success'.

While waiting for the owners to send new masts and spars from England, Learmont and his men made new sails . . . Then they set to work on the rigging. The *Bengairn* was said to look better than new when eventually she sailed again.

'You can lose a ship anywhere and in so many ways,' said Learmont, who had no time for the Newcastle coal trimmers. 'Fight the shore bastards and look after the ship *all the time*.'

How many missing ships did bad stowage account for? Newcastle was not alone in loading cargoes that shifted, and so many ships just vanished from the sea—leaving no survivors; no clues. They simply disappeared. Perhaps no absolutely fool-proof methods of stowage have ever been perfected. Cargoes can sink even the biggest vessels of today. Ballast, shifting in a squall, nearly sank the *Acamas* in 1903. It put paid to the *Dalgonar* in 1913. It was the death of so many ships, and when it happened it happened quickly. There was scant time to launch a lifeboat. Seldom was anyone left to tell the tale.

Nitrate was said to be a safe cargo. If properly stowed it 'set hard' and almost never shifted. Coal and grain were another matter. In a horrifying paper on ship losses, read before the Institute of Naval Architects in 1886,

Professor Francis Elgar stated that between 1881 and 1883, out of 264 British ships of over 300 tons that had gone missing without trace, 86 had been laden with coal and 44 with grain. And he linked this with the shifting of cargo in bad weather.

> We thus see that grain and coal cargoes account for one-half of the whole number of missing ships, and more than one-half of the whole number of lives lost (3,006); coal being responsible for one-third and grain for one-sixth . . .

Referring to other losses he pointed out that most coal-carrying vessels that foundered were lost with all hands, so that no details of their loss were available, but from the evidence of surviving crew members who abandoned ship it seemed that, in each case, the pumps became more or less inoperative through getting choked with small coal and dirt. So with grain-laden ships:

> Out of thirteen grain-laden ships lost . . . the whole of the thirteen went down with all hands, except for one vessel. In the case of that vessel, we find she was thrown upon her beam ends in a hurricane, the cargo shifted, water got below among the grain, the pumps ultimately became choked with grain, and the vessel had to be abandoned.

Nicholls's *Seamanship Guide* of 1905 has some interesting comments on cargo stowage. Apropos the loading of grain he says: 'No ship is allowed to

Date	Astoria (Oregon) to Channel for Orders	Days out
1895		
Jan. 21st	Left Astoria, grain cargo, *Departure* from C. Disappointment	
Jan. 30th	Ship sighted ahead and left out of sight astern same day	
Feb. 20th	Crossed Equator in Long. 118 West	30
March 9th	Crossed meridian of Cape Horn in Lat. 57 14 S.	47
March 10th	American ship 'Parthia' in company (heavy gale)	
April 3rd	Passed a barque and left her out of sight same day	
April 9th	Crossed Equator in long. 27½ West	78
May 11th	Sighted Cape Clear	110
May 12th	*Arrived Queenstown*, passage port to port Ship proceeded to Fleetwood to discharge grain cargo	111

load an entire cargo of grain in bulk unless specially constructed and loaded in accordance with a plan approved by the Board of Trade.'

This legislation must have followed a series of disasters.

But at the end of 1894 when William Nelson sailed the *Auchencairn* from San Francisco to Portland to load grain for Britain, neither Nicholls's comments nor Professor Elgar's paper had been published. At the time, William was only too pleased to have a cargo to load.

> From Frisco we went in ballast to Portland, Oregon (Astoria) and loaded grain for the U.K., sailing homeward on the 21st January,1895.
>
> We made splendid progress, passing Cape Horn 47 days out, and completing the passage from Astoria to Queenstown in 111 days, arriving on the 12th May.

VOYAGE 3

> The ship delivered her cargo at Fleetwood and then took on sailing ballast and sailed in tow of the tug *Black Cock* direct for Portland, Oregon, again. The tug was cast off on the 14th June, 1895 off the South Stack, whence our departure was taken.
>
> Outward bound, we sighted more than one incoming vessel *which had left the Pacific coast ahead of us*, on our recent homeward passage! Seeing us, and not yet having completed their homeward runs, they must have done a lot of hard thinking!

With what glee William must have written the preceding paragraph. To overhaul ships that started weeks ahead of him he had done before. We have come to expect it of him. But to sail home, discharge his cargo, take on ballast and then set off again only to pass the same ships still on their homeward run—that is fantastic. How the tongues must have wagged aboard those incoming ships as, one by one, the crews sighted the *Auchencairn* blithely sailing westwards on her new voyage. Small wonder that William Andrew Nelson had become a legend. News travelled fast in the seaports of those days.

> We passed Cape Horn 59 days out and arrived off Cape Disappointment off Columbia River 116 days out from Holyhead (departure), and berthed the following day. Not a bad passage for rounding the Horn in ballast. Date of docking, 9th October, 1895.

Date	Fleetwood to Portland, Oregon	Days out
1895		
June 13th	Left Fleetwood in ballast, towed by tug 'Black Cock'	
June 14th	Cast off tug and took *departure* from the South Stack	
June 16th	Sighted many homeward bounders steering by the wind, one or two of these ships had left the Pacific coast before us and were only to the chops of the channel when we were sailing outward	
June 24th	Passed two barques bound same way	
July 2nd	Spoke ship 'Romanoff' of Aberdeen from* London to Sydney, 21 days out	18
July 7th to 10th	Passed several vessels bound same way	
July 14th	Crossed Equator in Long. 27 West	30
July 22nd	Spoke barque 'Janet McNeil' from Weymouth to Chile, 48 days out	38
July 25th	Passed a ship bound same way, left her out of sight same day.	
Aug. 12th	Passed Diego Ramirez (Cape Horn)	59
Aug. 27th	Passed a 4-masted ship in ballast bound same way	
Sept. 9th	Crossed Equator (Pacific) in Long. 110 West	87
Sept. 29th	Exchanged longitudes with S.S. 'Miowera'	
Oct. 8th	Sighted Cape Disappointment Light	116
Oct. 9th	*Arrived* in berth. Passage from departure to Portland	117

*Ship 'Romanoff' was signalled on April 4th, 1889 by me in 'William Ritson'

Years later, Thomas Benn of Maryport (see p. 102), who sailed on that voyage, said: 'Willie Nelson wasn't a man for wasting time on a passage. He wouldn't give away an inch to windward. I remember when we were close-hauled off the Horn. The wind was rising and the *Auchencairn* was thrashing along into heavy seas and sticking her nose in it. Just at dark the Old Man comes up from the cabin half-way through his dinner, looks at the sky and says to the mate: "We'll shorten sail. Take the flying-jib and fore-top-staysail off her." And goes below again.

'Well, after he's finished eating, he comes up on deck and finds the sails still set. "What's happening?" he asks. "The crew don't want to go out on the jib-boom with all that sea coming over", says the mate. "They're waiting for

Built at Maryport, the *Ladas* was named after Lord Rosebery's racehorse which won the Derby in 1894.
Captain W. A. Nelson was her last master during her ownership by Messrs Ritsons.

Barque *Inverness* off Beachy Head, painted by Captain James Nelson who served in her. She was built of steel (1959 tons), for George Milne and Co. of Aberdeen, by McMillans of Dumbarton in 1902. Milnes believed in making their men comfortable, so she was given a much finer fo'c'sle than was usual in those days, and she had the reputation of having the best half-deck in the Milne fleet.

you to square-away." "Square-away! I'm not squaring-away," says Willie Nelson—and goes marching for'ard. "What's all this about?" he says to the crew. "Have I got to get out there and stow those sails myself?"

'And they knew he could. And they knew he would. And they weren't going to have that talked about in Maryport! There was no more argument after that. It was who could get out on that jib-boom first!

'He'd keep a ship at top speed day and night, would Captain Willie. The only time I ever saw him in two minds whether to heave-to was near the start of a passage, when he came up on deck and his new sou'wester blew overboard . . . But it sank!'

In tow of the tug *Relief*, we left again on the 3rd November, bound to U.K. with a cargo of grain and cast off tug the same day. Thus we had the

Date	Portland Oregon to Channel for Orders	Days out
1895		
Nov. 3rd	Left Portland in tow of tug 'Relief', grain cargo. *Departure*	
Nov. 5th	Four barques passed bound to the Northward	
Nov. 26th	Crossed Equator (Pacific) in Long. 108 West	23
Dec. 10th	Passed a barque bound same way, supposed 'Beeswing' and a 5-masted schooner.	
Dec. 25th	Xmas day, spoke barque 'Prince Amadeo' from Vancouver to Halifax, 66 days out	52
Dec. 26th	Passed meridian of Cape Horn in Lat. 57 56 S. sighted two large and several small ice-bergs	53
Dec. 27th	Spoke 4-masted ship 'Andromeda' from Portland, Oregon, 70 days out, strong NNE gale	54
Dec. 31st	Spoke ship 'Kinkora' Frisco to Cork 58 days out	58
1896		
Jan. 1st	'Kinkora' dropped out of sight to leeward	
Jan 26th	Crossed Equator (Atlantic) in Long. 25 West, spoke barque 'Chilena' from Guadelope	84
Feb. 19th	Ship 'Wallacetown' sent boat alongside requesting provisions, 2nd mate reported ship leaking badly and short of food, 119 days out from Junin, Chile.	
March 2nd	Made land fall near Galley Head	120
March 3rd	*Arrived Queenstown* – passage from port to port	121

distinction of leaving Portland, Oregon, with a second cargo for England in
the space of 9½ months—a record rarely equalled.

But not only has William done some wonderful sailing, he keeps it up . . .

This time, although we were 53 days to the Horn we had not done so badly, for
on 27th December, in spite of having been impeded by several icebergs, we
overhauled and passed the four-master *Andromeda*, which was then 70 days
out from Portland.

The *Andromeda* had started sixteen days ahead of him!

North of the 'Line' the ship *Wallacetown* sent his boat over to us. The second
mate reported she was leaking badly; that they were 119 days out from Junin
(Chile) and short of provisions. We gave them all the stores we could spare,
and soon left her astern.

From the Equator to the Channel there were poor winds, which added
about a week to my usual passage. We made Cape Clear 120 days out and
arrived at Queenstown on the following day, 3rd March, 1896.

Following orders at Queenstown, we proceeded to Antwerp to discharge
and made a remarkably fast run, sailing from Queenstown to Flushing in 35
hours. Distance, about 480 miles. Average speed, nearly 14 knots.

VOYAGE 4

Date	Port Pirie to San Francisco	Days out
1896		
Sept. 4th	Sailed from Port Pirie, cargo not mentioned	
Sept. 8th	Off Cape Otway, several days of light airs and calms	
Sept. 10th	Passed Wilson's Promontory, took *Departure*	
Sept. 18th	Sighted Three Kings Islets off North end New Zealand	8
Sept. 20th	Passed a 4-masted ship during night and left her astern	
Oct. 22nd	Crossed Equator in Long. 121 West	42
Nov. 6th	Spoke 4-masted barque 'Bracadale' from Newcastle N.S.W. to San Francisco, 81 days out, and dropped her astern	57
Nov. 7th	Passed and spoke 4-masted barque 'Crown of Germany' from Panama, 65 days out. Passed four other vessels bound the same way	
Nov. 10th	*Arrived San Francisco*—passage from departure	61

The grain cargo having been discharged at Antwerp, the ship loaded for Port Pirie, sailing from Antwerp on the 8th May, 1896. Taking our departure from Prawle Point on the 10th May, we crossed the Equator 27 days out.

From Lat. 31½ South, Long. 18.45 West we did some good sailing to Kangaroo Island, practically our destination, doing the 7,105 miles in 31 days.

From the same position to Lat. 41.25 South, Long. 111.40 East, we ran 6,072 miles in 25 days, an *average* speed of about 10.3 knots.

The passage to Kangaroo Island was made in 71 days; 74 days to destination.

The *Auchencairn*'s daily runs for the twenty-five days between 19th June and 14th July were: 228, 214, 216, 230, 220, 238, 240, 220, 234, 225, 233, 240, 225, 220, 301, 253, 170, 278, 288, 294, 266, 280, 283, 230, 246. Total: 6,072 miles. Some very fine long-distance sailing.

From Port Pirie* the ship proceeded direct to San Francisco. Leaving Port Pirie on the 4th September, 1896, we made rather slow progress while working down the Spencer Gulf owing to very light head winds, and calms.

We took our departure off Wilson's Promontory on the 10th September, and made a good passage to San Francisco in 61 days. On the 6th November we overhauled and passed the four-masted barque *Bracadale* of Glasgow, which was then 81 days out from Newcastle NSW, against our 57 days out from Wilson's Promontory. The following day we passed and spoke the four-masted barque *Crown of Germany* from Panama, 65 days out. Later, we passed four other vessels bound the same way.

We arrived at San Francisco on 10th November.

Having loaded a cargo of grain, bound to Channel for orders, we sailed from San Francisco on the 15th January, 1897 in tow of the tug *Vigilant*, casting off the tug and taking our departure the same day.

Good sailing was done to Cape Horn. (We crossed the Equator 19 days out; sighted Ducie Island, in about Lat. 25 South, 31 days out, and passed Cape Horn 49 days out.)

Our progress from the Horn to the Channel was not so good, owing to contrary winds and calms, nevertheless we overhauled and passed a great many

*The *Auchencairn*'s log for the passage Antwerp to Port Pirie reads: 'July 23rd. Arrived Port Germein'. This port, which is marked on the original chart of Australia by Captain Matthew Flinders, is 11 miles north of Port Pirie. It was he, incidentally, who named Kangaroo Island—having found an abundance of these animals when stopping there to provision while on his exploratory voyage. In charting Australia, Flinders was the first person to discover Bass Strait, and thus that Tasmania is an island and not part of the mainland—which Captain Cook and others had believed. Although Flinders returned to England with his charts in 1801, a map published in 1810 still shows Tasmania (named Van Diemen's Land) as a promontory, not an island. Bass Strait was named after Dr Bass, who accompanied Flinders on his voyage.

Date	San Francisco to Channel for orders	Days out
1897		
Jan. 15th	Left Frisco in tow tug 'Vigilant', *Departure* same day	
Feb. 3rd	Crossed Equator (Pacific) in Long. 119 West	19
Feb. 15th	Sighted Ducie Island, Lat. 24 40 S. Long. 124 48 W	31
March 5th	Passed Cape Horn	49
March 12th	Spoke barque 'Rockhurst' of London from Astoria to Wisbech, 77 days out	56
March 24th	Spoke ship 'Euterpe' of Southampton from Wellington	
April 1st	After six days of light winds 'Rockhurst' sighted coming up astern, but dropped out of sight astern when wind came	
April 7th	Crossed Equator (Atlantic) in Long. 26 West	82
April 8th	Spoke German barque 'Marie' steering South	
April 9th	Four masted ship and four other vessels in company	
April 11th	Four masted ship and seven other vessels in company	
April 13th	Four masted ship dropped out of sight. Spoke ship 'Socotra' from San Francisco 118 days out	88
April 15th	Spoke and passed ship 'Perseverance' of Glasgow from Astoria, 121 days out	90
April 17th	Spoke ship 'Glenfinart' from Frisco 91 days out	92
May 1st	Spoke barque 'Criffel' from Astoria 147 days	106
May 7th	Thirteen homeward bound ships in company	
May 8th	Spoke four masted ship 'Doisan Hill' Spoke ship 'Norman McCleod' from Wellington 94 days out Spoke ship 'Drumpark' from Port Pirie, 125 days out	
May 9th	Lat. 47 N. Long. 27 West, *26 sailing ships in sight*	
May 10th	Number of sail in sight reduced to eight	
May 14th	Off Cape Clear	119
May 15th	Arrived Queenstown—passage port to port	120

homeward-bounders—having taken a month out of a few from the Pacific coast. For example, at the time of signalling we were 30 days ahead of the Socotra from Frisco; 41 days ahead of the *Criffel* from Astoria; 31 days ahead of the *Perseverance* from Astoria. These vessels were spoken north of the Equator. We had been 21 days ahead of the *Rockhurst* from Astoria and spoken off the Falkland Islands. The only ship that kept pace with us was the *Glenfinart* from Frisco.

This is rather surprising. Like her sister '*Glens*', the *Glenfinart*—a 1,963 ton steel ship built in 1895 by Messrs A. Rodger & Co. of Port Glasgow—had no reputation for speed; whereas the *Criffel*—built in Maryport by Ritsons and launched in 1891, the same year as the *Auchencairn*—was (like a sister ship, the *Ladas*) considered a very fine specimen of the 1,300–1,400 ton barque.

> We sighted an exceptional number of sail between the Line and the Channel—probably due to the persistent light and variable winds. On 9th May, in Lat. 47 North, Long. 27 West, we actually counted 26 sailing ships. A wonderful sight. Among these, we exchanged signals with the *Doisan Hill*; *Norman McCleod*; *Drumpark*, and an Italian ship. A breeze made during the night, and the following day saw this unarmed armada of sail reduced to eight ships.
>
> On 14th May we arrived off Cape Clear and berthed the next morning, having made a passage well above the average: 119 days from Frisco.
>
> This was destined to be the last voyage of the *Auchencairn* under the Red Ensign. We proceeded to Limerick to discharge. There the ship was sold to a Bremen firm and renamed *Nomia*. She continued to sail under the German flag until she went missing on a passage from Newcastle NSW to the West Coast of Chile in 1912. Her master was Captain Himme.

James Nelson recalled seeing his father's old ship some years later. 'About October, 1908, I was in Limerick, 2nd mate of barque *Inverness*, when the *Nomia* arrived and made fast alongside. The mate told me that the old *Auchencairn* continued to make good passages.

'She remained under the German flag and went missing on passage from Newcastle NSW to West Coast of Chile with *coal* cargo.' (My italics)

Significant, that coal. Did it shift, I wonder, as her coal shifted in September 1894? And if so, this time did she turn right over?

To illustrate the consistently good sailing of the *Auchencairn* under William Nelson's captaincy, here are some *average* times:

Outward bound from Channel to Pacific coast ports	117 days
Homeward from Pacific Coast ports to U.K.	115 days
Outward to Cape Horn	60½ days
Equator, Atlantic to Equator, Pacific	62 days
Homeward, Pacific ports to Cape Horn	50 days
Equator, Pacific to Equator, Atlantic	57 days
Greatest variation in times of homeward runs	10 days
Variation in times of outward runs (two only)	1 day
Two passages across the Pacific from Australia:	
Port Pirie to San Francisco	64 days
Newcastle to San Francisco	61 days

After handing over the *Auchencairn* to her new (German) owners, William returned to Maryport to watch his next command fitting-out at Messrs Ritsons' yard. This was to be another famous vessel: the full-rigged ship *Acamas*.

Thomas Benn AB, Maryport fisherman and lifeboat coxwain who was in the *Auchencairn* on that epic voyage is discharged at Antwerp.

There is no record of how and when he returned to Maryport; but whatever the story, it is not likely to better the tale Tom Leece told me about Tom Benn's father, John Benn AB. It is typical of the happy-go-lucky attitude of the 19th century sailor, before the days of telephones and telegrams.

'At the end of a voyage in 1860, John had been paid-off—in sovereigns. Twenty he'd got. He put them in his money-belt: Reckoned he'd catch the train to Maryport in the morning. Left his dunnage-bag in the Seamen's Mission and went to the boozer.

'He woke up next morning remembering nothing except that he had to get back to his wife in Maryport. But he had a terrible thirst, and his coppers were hot.* So, he shoulders his bag and goes to the boozer for a glass of rum before catching his train.

*An old seaman's expression for 'money burning a hole in the pocket'.

'The rum cost 4d. John feels in his belt and gives the barman what he thinks is a sovereign.

'The barman gives him 8d change.

'John seizes the barman's wrist. "I gave you a sovereign. You owe me nineteen shillings!"

'"If you can find a sovereign in this bar you can have it", says the barman. "You gave me a shilling."

'John examines the contents of his money-belt. Only a few shilling pieces. Someone, it seems, has robbed him while he slept, substituting shillings for sovereigns to allay suspicion. John was done for. Twenty sovereigns was a fortune in those days. He couldn't go back home with no money. Nothing for it but to get another ship and go back to sea.

'John takes up his bag and goes down to the dock. A ship is just leaving. He signs on.

'The voyage was a long one. Two years later, John Benn returns to Liverpool and gets paid-off.

'This time he takes no chances. It's the first train to Maryport.

'"Where've *you* been to?" asks Mrs Benn.

'"Back to sea," says John. "I was robbed the voyage before. I had to get another ship."

'"You great fool!" says his wife. "You weren't robbed. It was the Minister at the Mission. He found you drunk. Took your money for safe keeping. Left you with some shillings for drink. He was waiting for you in the morning to get you some breakfast, but you never turned up. In the end, he sent me the money."

'John Benn was so shaken he never went on a long voyage again. After that he stuck to the coasting trade out of Maryport.'

15

The *Acamas*

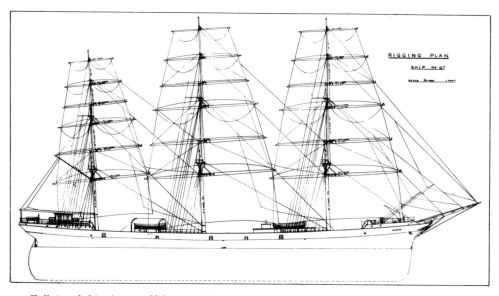

Full rigged ship *Acamas* of Maryport. Nett tons: 1715. Gross tons: 1862. Length OA: 309 ft. Beam: 39 ft. Fore-mast, truck to main deck: 140 ft. Mainmast, truck to main deck: 145 ft. Mizzenmast, truck to main deck: 120 ft.

VOYAGE I

The *Acamas*, although without the lofty appearance of the older ships, carried a great spread of canvas. The fore and main yards measured 90 feet, the royal yards 40 feet. The mainmast reached 145 feet from deck to truck. She was fitted with double topgallant yards on each mast, thus spreading six square sails to each mast. Her lines were rather full, which made her a big carrier, and a good seaboat, but reduced her sailing qualities. Her hull was painted in the same style as the *Auchencairn* with black ports on a white band. Below this she was painted French grey. Then came the red boot-topping.

Abstracts from log of ship 'Acamas', Voyage 1; Capt. W. A. Nelson
(ACAMAS—Son of Theseus, went with Diomede to rescue Helen from the
Trojans. Joined in the Trojan War.)

Date	Newport Mon to Geraldton, Australia	Days out
1897		
Oct. 3rd	Left Newport, cargo steel rails, in tow tug 'Glenrosa'	
Oct. 4th	Cast off tug and took *departure* from Lundy Island	
Oct. 20th	Sighted Cape St Antonio, Cape Verde Isles	16
Oct. 21st	Four masted ship been in company 4 days goes ahead of us	
Oct. 26th	Ship 'Champion' drops astern, been in company 10 days	
Oct. 31st	Crossed Equator in Long. 27½ West	27
Nov. 17th	Sighted Tristan D'Cunha Island	44
Nov. 27th	Crossed meridian Cape Aghulas in Lat. 44½ S.	54
Dec. 21st	Arrived off Geraldton (Diverted to Fremantle)	78
	Total distance sailed by noon to noon positions, 12,432 miles	

Date	Newcastle, N.S.W. to San Francisco	Days out
1898		
Apr. 17th	Left Newcastle in tow, coal cargo, cast off tug, *Departure*	
May 24th	Crossed Equator in Long. 105 West	37
June 28th	*Arrived* San Francisco, passage port to port	72
	Total distance sailed, noon to noon, 8,245 miles	

On completion we towed to Newport, Monmouth. There we loaded a cargo of railway iron for Geraldton, Australia, and sailed in tow of the tug *Glenrosa* on the 3rd October, 1897. With Lundy Island abeam the tug was cast off and our departure taken.

For 10 days we sailed in company with the ship *Champion*, and then dropped her astern, crossing the Equator 27 days out.

After an uneventful passage we arrived off Geraldton 78 days out. There we got diverted to Newcastle NSW.

At Newcastle we loaded coal for San Francisco. We sailed on 17th April, and made the passage in 72 days.

From Frisco we sailed in ballast to Steveston on the Fraser River in British Columbia, where a full cargo of canned salmon was loaded for Liverpool.

On 10th October, 1898 we sailed in tow of the tug *Pioneer*, and the following day took our departure from Cape Flattery.

On making sail I found that with this particular cargo the ship was crank. This was disappointing, as it meant that she would not stand much driving. In consequence, I made my longest passage home from the Pacific coast: 139 days to the Tuskar Rock, arriving in dock at Liverpool the following day.

Thus ended the maiden voyage of the *Acamas*. Quite uneventful.

Date	Steveston, B.C. (Frazer River) to Liverpool	Days out
1898		
Oct. 10th	Left in tow tug 'Pioneer', cargo canned salmon	
Oct. 11th	Cast off tug 8 miles off Cape Flattery, *Depature*.	
Nov. 7th	Crossed Equator (Pacific) in Long. 124 West	27
Dec. 17th	Crossed Meridian Cape Horn in Lat. 57 South	67
1899		
Jan. 28th	Crossed Equator in Long. 28 50 West	109
Feb. 15th	Carried away fore topgallant mast in squall	
Feb. 27th	Sighted Tuskar Light, passage from Cape Flattery	139
Feb. 28th	Anchored in River Mersey	140
	Total distance sailed, 16,678 miles	

Uneventful, yes—apart from the loss of the fore topgallant mast. This incident is not mentioned in William's memoirs, but is included in the ship's log.

'Feb 15th. Carried away fore topgallant mast in squall.'

That topgallant mast was 30 feet in length. The royal mast above it was 17 feet. Both were made of steel. In addition, there were the steel yards of the three sails from those masts. The lower topgallant yard, 61 feet. The upper topgallant yard, 52½ feet. The royal yard, 40 feet. Over 150 feet of steel spars together with 47 feet of steel masts were swinging about aloft, clanging against the standing foremast and threatening with every roll of the ship to cause further damage. Handling steel spars was a very different proposition from handling wood. Cutting away that wreckage and stowing it safely must have taken a lot of time, not to mention some skilled and dangerous work.

But William doesn't mention it. I sense his frustration. As he wrote, he was disappointed. He didn't like the way the *Acamas* was carrying those tins of salmon. She was 'crank'. That is, she was tender—due to the cargo's centre of gravity being fractionally too high—and so wouldn't stand much driving. And to a seaman as finely tuned to fast sailing as William, this must have been irritating.

Anyway, north of the Equator he found a slant of wind and tried to make her sail. And she wouldn't. And I think that for once he hung on too long—and it rankled.

VOYAGE 2

Abstracts from log of ship 'Acamas', Voyage 2; Capt. W. A. Nelson

Date	Liverpool to Calcutta	Days out
1899		
Apr. 13th	Left Liverpool in tow tug 'Hotspur', Cargo Salt	
Apr. 13th	Cast off tug off Holyhead, strong Southerly	
Apr. 14th	*Departure* from Tuskar Lt., barques 'Trongate' and 'Metropolis' and one Norwegian in company	
Apr. 16th	Lost sight of above vessels during night	
May 6th	Sighted Cape Antonio, Cape Verde Isles	22
May 12th	Spoke ship 'Torridan' London to Sydney, 36 days out	28
May 18th	Crossed Equator (Atlantic) in Long. 22 40 W.	34
June 16th	Thunder bolt or meteor fell near ship, same moment a gust of wind split main and mizzen upper and lower topsails	
June 21st	Crossed meridian of Cape Aghulas in Lat. 41 S.	68
July 18th	Crossed Equator in Long. 82 East (Indian Ocean)	95
July 27th	*Arrived* off River Hooghly and took steam	104
	Total distance sailed, reckoning from noon to noon, 14,497 miles	

The second voyage started on the 13th April, 1899, when we sailed with a cargo of salt for Calcutta in tow of the tug *Hotspur*.

The 13th seemed to be living up to its evil reputation, for by the time we cast off the tug off the South Stack, the barometer had dropped to 28.80 and it was blowing a whole gale from the southward. However, after a very dirty night the glass began to rise and the wind veered to the westward.

In company with the barques *Trongate* and *Metropolis*, we took our departure from the Tuskar Light. During the following night the 'convoy' dispersed and we did not sight each other again on the voyage.

On 16th June, when about to round the Cape of Good Hope, we had the startling experience of a thunderbolt dropping very close to the ship. At the same time, a sudden gust of wind split the upper and lower topsails on both main and mizzen.

Date	Calcutta to Hamburg	Days out
1899		
Nov. 16th	Sailed in tow tug 'Hooghly', 5 p.m. anchored at Calpee	
Nov. 17th	6 a.m. underway in tow, 5 p.m. Cast off tug, no wind and flood tide, anchored	
Nov. 18th	6 a.m. Got underway and made all sail, light airs, *Departure*	
Dec. 1st	Crossed Equator (Indian Ocean) in Long. 85 E.	13
1900		
Jan. 4th	Sighted Cape of Good Hope, East 12 miles dist.	47
Jan. 16th	Sighted St. Helena Island . . . 3 miles off	59
Jan. 27th	Crossed Equator (Atlantic) in long. 25 West	70
Jan. 31st	Spoke barque 'Doris', New York to Australia	
Feb. 24th	Sighted Casquettes, South 16 miles	98
Feb. 25th	Off Dungeness at midnight	99
Feb. 28th	*Arrived* River Elbe, passage port to port	102
	Total distance sailed 14,185 miles	

It is not clear quite what William meant by a 'thunderbolt dropping very close to the ship'. Was it a lightning flash—the usual meaning of 'thunderbolt', or something more substantial? In the log he writes: 'thunderbolt or meteor', implying that a *meteorite* had plunged into the sea close alongside.

If this was really the case the ship's company had a lucky escape, for had a meteorite struck the *Acamas* it would certainly have sunk her. The chances of such a thing happening must be (literally) astronomical! Nevertheless, had the *Acamas* gone missing her loss would be listed as yet another of those 'Mysteries of the Sea'.

It is sobering reflection that whatever it was William logged on the 16th June, 1899, the accompanying 'sudden gust of wind' must have been exceptionally fierce to have split main and mizzen topsails—most of the ship's storm canvas.

We arrived and took steam off the Hooghly estuary, 104 days out from the Tuskar.

On 16th November, 1899, we left Calcutta with a cargo of jute for Hamburg in tow of the tug *Hooghly* and anchored for the night at Calpee, proceeding in tow the following day until 5 pm, when the tug was cast off. But as there was no wind, and a flood tide was running we anchored.

The following day we got underway with a light breeze and took our departure on the 18th November.

We sighted the Cape of Good Hope 47 days out, and St Helena 59 days out, arriving off Dungeness after 99 days, and finally arriving in the River Elbe 102 days from Calcutta.

So, on the 28th February, 1900, ended the second voyage.

VOYAGE 3

Abstracts from log of ship 'Acamas', Voyage 3; Capt. W. A. Nelson

Date	Hamburg to San Francisco	Days out
1900		
May 4th	Left Hamburg in tow, general cargo	
May 5th	Cleared River Elbe and later cast off tug	
May 11th	Signalled Prawle Point, took *Departure*	
June 5th	Crossed Equator (Atlantic) in Long. 24 West	25
June 15th	Spoke German steamer 'Memphis'	
July 14th	Off Cape Horn, Fresh N.N.E. wind	64
Aug. 11th	Crossed Equator (Pacific) in Long. 112 West	92
Sept. 13th	*Arrived* San Francisco, passage from Prawle Point	125
	Total distance sailed, 16,612 miles	

The third voyage of the *Acamas* started on the 4th May, 1900, sailing from Hamburg with a general cargo consigned to San Francisco. Our departure was taken from Prawle Point on the 11th May.

The outward passage was made in 125 days. We arrived on the 13th September.

From San Francisco we returned with a cargo of grain bound to the Channel for orders, sailing on the night of the 3rd November and casting off the tug early the next morning.

The only vessel spoken on the passage was the outward-bound ship *Celtic Queen*, 47 days out from Hamburg to Iquique, on the 6th January, 1901.

On the 7th March, 1901, we sighted the Wolf Lighthouse and arrived Falmouth the same day, having been 124 days on the homeward run.

From Falmouth we proceeded to Hull to discharge. This ended voyage 3.

Date	San Francisco to Channel for orders	Days out
1900		
Nov. 3rd	P.M. sailed in tow, cargo grain.	
Nov. 4th	A.M. cast off tug and took *Departure*	
Nov. 28th	Crossed Equator (Pacific) in long. 124½ West	24
Dec. 25th	Xmas Day, Passed Cape Horn in Lat. 56½ South, gale and rain	51
1901		
Jan. 6th	Spoke ship 'Celtic Queen', Hamburg to Iquique 47 days out	
Feb. 1st	Crossed Equator (Atlantic) in long. 25½ West	89
Feb. 5th	Passed a four-masted barque bound same way	
Mar. 7th	Sighted Wolf Rock and *arrived* Falmouth same day	124
	Total distance sailed, 15,554 miles	

Looking back over William's memoirs and reading the logs he kept since taking command of the *Acamas*, it is significant how little he has to say about these remarkable voyages. Four years, from 1897 to 1901, spent thrashing round the world, are dismissed in two or three brief pages. And yet they represent nearly 100,000 miles of the hardest sailing. The only 'incidents' recorded are the loss of a topgallant mast and a 'thunderbolt' that splits his topsails.

It is, of course, because they are so incident-free that these voyages are so remarkable. At sea, the best story of all concerns the passage with 'no story in it'. But over the same period as this and on passages similar to those made by the *Acamas*, ship after ship was lost or badly damaged. Log books were full of disasters; of crew troubles. Bad landfalls were made. Ships collided. Ships were dismasted, wrecked, abandoned, sunk. Ships caught fire. Ships simply disappeared . . . But William has sailed the *Acamas* nearly four times the distance round the Earth in fast, safe passages, with no sign in his log book of the troubles that beset so many 'limejuicers' of the period. It all has the stamp of supreme professionalism; of a well-disciplined ship and a properly-fed and contented crew.

VOYAGE 4

I think it was the Watkins tug *Guiana* that towed the ship from Hull to Barry. On the 18th May, 1901, the fourth voyage started when we sailed from Barry Dock with a cargo of coal and coke for Port Pirie. The tug was cast off at Lundy Island in light airs and dense fog, our departure being taken on the 20th May, from the sound of the fog-signal on the Seven Stones Lightship.

On 29th May, we came up on the barque *Tinto Hill* bound from Cardiff to Algoa Bay and 14 days out against our 11 from Barry.

On 15th August we sighted the Neptune Island and arrived at Port Germain on the following day, having been 88 days on passage to destination.

We left Port Pirie in ballast for Newcastle NSW with a light fair wind. Soon however, the wind came ahead and we had a trying time beating down the Spencer Gulf, which meant my presence on deck most of the time. I remember going down to my cabin about 2 am to consult the chart—and unintentionally fell asleep in my chair.

I awoke about dawn and hurried on deck only to find the faint outline of Spilsby Island close aboard on the lee bow. I immediately gave the order to 'wear ship' but before she got round she took the ground and remained fast.

Having tried all methods known to seamen to refloat her, but without success, I sent the boat away in charge of the second mate, telling him to search for a telegraph station and send a message to Adelaide for a tug.

After a long pull and search the second mate got the message through, and in due course a tug arrived.

It might as well have stayed in Adelaide for all the use it was. For a day or two it made a few feeble efforts to refloat the ship, after which, as it had made not the slightest impression, I sent it away. Later the same day a fine breeze came right off-shore and I set all the sails aback. To my delight the ship came straight off, stern first, and fortune favoured us even further when we narrowly missed hitting some rocks as she made her stern board.

The ship was not leaking, but I put into Adelaide for survey and to be certified as seaworthy. Sure enough, on dry-docking we found no damage, only the paint chafed. However, I was hauled up before a court of enquiry composed of a few old cronies most of whom had not been to sea for ages and knew more about greengrocery stores. I was severely censured for not having left more explicit orders with the officer on watch. They had little to say about my getting the ship off where the local tug had failed.

Abstracts from log of ship 'Acamas', Voyage 4; Capt. W. A. Nelson

Date	Barry Dock to Port Pirie	Days out
1901		
May 18th	Left Barry in tow, cargo coal/coke	
May 19th	Cast off tug off Lundy Island. Light airs and misty	
May 20th	*Departure* from fog-signal on Seven Stones Lt/ship	
May 29th	Spoke 4-masted barque 'Tinto Hill', from Cardiff to Algoa Bay, 14 days out	9
June 1st	Six vessels in company	
June 23rd	Crossed Equator in long. 26½ West	34
July 19th	Crossed meridian of Cape Aghulas in Lat. 42 South	60
Aug. 15th	Passed Neptune Islands and arrived Spencer Gulf	87
Aug. 16th	*Arrived* at Port Germain	88
	Total distance sailed on passage 13,575 miles.	

William was always scathing about his being censured by the Australian 'greengrocers'—but it hurt. He felt there was something odd about that grounding; that it shouldn't have happened. As it transpired, he was right—although he never knew why. The truth came out quite by chance long after his death.

In March, 1946, Captain James Nelson met an old friend and shipmate, Captain 'Robbie' Robson, who was then Harbour Master at Immingham and on the point of retirement. He had been an apprentice in the *Acamas* and was aboard her when she went aground. Reminiscing about this, Captain Robson divulged a secret which, until then, he had kept all his life. On the night the *Acamas* grounded he and another boy had been sent to clean the brasswork on the Standard Compass, situated on top of the half-deck (the compass used for

The *Mary Moore* at Melbourne, photographed by Captain James Nelson in 1934. Hulked in 1906 she
continued in use for 50 years.

The harbour at Iquique, about 1880.

The *Brier Holme* was lost with only one survivor off the Tasmanian coast in 1904.

Vallejo and Broadway wharves, San Francisco harbour, towards the end of the nineteenth century.

Captain John Rich, master of the three-masted barque *Brier Holme* of Maryport, photographed in London before his last voyage.

In or near port, the great windjammers, like the *Hougomont* shown here at Maryport (in 1903), were helpless without the steam tug. Even so, it seemed impossible that steam, created by costly coal, could ever replace wind-power. But even when this picture was taken, the days of sail were virtually over.

The harbour at Portland, Oregon in about 1880 and (*below*) in 1899.

Acamas on the stocks in Messrs Ritsons' yard beside the little River Ellen, nearly ready for her launching in 1897. Maryport Harbour and waterfront lie just beyond the bridge; and beyond the distant harbour mole, the Solway Firth.

The crew of the *Acamas*, San Francisco, 1903. James Nelson, captain to be, then apprentice on his father's ship, is second from right, back row.

Captain and Mrs W. A. Nelson at Queenstown, May 1905, shortly before the start of the *Acamas*'s epic voyage from Port Talbot to Pisagua.

Fitting out one of the new Maryport steel-built 'working ships'.

The barque *Ladas* when under the ownership of Rasmus F. Olsen.

Retired but undiminished.

Ninety, but still the same undaunted look.

Maryport in 1900. The twin-paddle steamer *Manxman* leaving on a day trip to the Isle of Man. Smoke billows from the funnels as the vessel passes admiring crowds. A new era is under way and the days of sail are almost over.

taking bearings!). Bored with their work, the lads forced open the binnacle door and amused themselves by removing the correction magnets and making the compass card swing about. The magnets were wrongly replaced and, unknown to William Nelson, when the ship touched Spilsby Island the Bearing Compass had an error of some three points.

At the time, however, all ended well and with a Certificate of Seaworthiness the *Acamas* left Adelaide for Newcastle NSW to load a cargo of coal.

Date	Newcastle N.S.W to Valparaiso	Days out
Dec. 1st	Left Newcastle, cargo coal, cast off tug same day, *Departure*	
Dec. 15th	Sighted Stewart Island, Lat. 47 40 S. Long. 167 10 E	14
Dec. 18th	Crossed 180th meridian in Lat. 45½ South	17
1902		
Jan. 15th	*Arrived* Valparaiso	45
	Total distance sailed on passage 6,571 miles	

On 1st December, 1901, we sailed from Newcastle for Valparaiso. The passage was uneventful, and we made the run in 45 days.

From Valparaiso we went in ballast to Taltal.

At Taltal we loaded saltpetre for Rotterdam. I have no record of this passage, but we arrived home in July. End of Voyage 4.

Taltal to Rotterdam

No trace of the log of this passage. The run took about 100 days

William's memory seems to have failed him over happenings at the end of that passage. But his surviving daughter, Margaret, remembers. She and her mother with two of her sisters joined the *Acamas* as the vessel sailed up-Channel to Rotterdam and thence to Cardiff. She writes:

My mother did not go often to sea, but used to join the ship at Falmouth or Queenstown or wherever, and sail on with her from there. At the end of Father's passage from Taltal she and I and the twins were aboard the *Acamas* when she sailed from Rotterdam to Cardiff to load a new cargo for Algoa Bay. It was terribly rough, and off Land's End the weather was so bad that the ship was actually reported 'lost with all hands'! However, we got safely into Cardiff, where we received a hero's welcome; but the pilot's boat nearly capsized three times before he got aboard and the apprentices told mother later that all the crew were praying!

It was on that passage, just as we were approaching Land's End, that a very unhappy incident occurred. Besides his little dog, 'Rock', that for years used to sail with him, Father had a semi-wild cat that came aboard the ship in Australia. Father had a great way with animals and was the only one who could feed this cat. It wouldn't go near anyone else. It lived in the storeroom and a porthole was always left open for it to hide away there. If anyone but Father appeared on the quarterdeck it would leap from the poop to the storeroom and stay out of sight. Well, on this occasion, as we were rounding Land's End, my mother appeared suddenly on deck, and because of the strong wind was wearing an 'Aberdeen Bannock'—a large Tam o' Shanter. The cat took one look at her, leapt off the poop and was never seen again. Whether it misjudged its leap, or the ship gave a sudden roll, I don't know. But overboard it went. Father was much upset.

VOYAGE 5

On the 29th September, 1902, the 5th voyage started when we left Barry with a cargo of coal for Algoa Bay. But when the tug *Flying Cormorant* came under the counter off Lundy Island to collect our mail and bid us a fond adieu (not forgetting his bottle and plug of tobacco) little did we think that we were embarking on a world cruise lasting 2 years and 9 months.

Owing to light winds we were 34 days to the Equator, where we sighted the four-masted barque *Torresdale*, which had left the Bristol Channel about the same time and was also bound for Algoa Bay. There was another small barque outward bound we took to be the *Atacama*, or one of the same company.

A few days before we left Barry there had been 'head-line' news in the papers describing a great gale which had swept Algoa Bay and wrecked a number of sailing ships. This gave us something to talk about on the passage.

We sailed into Algoa Bay and anchored four miles offshore, having been 61 days on the passage. The *Torresdale* took about the same time.

Sure enough the beach was strewn with wrecks. In one particular place there were five ships bunched together with their fallen spars intermingled. Most of the wrecked ships hailed from Scandinavia, only two British ships having been lost: the *Inchcape Rock* and another vessel. Among the ships anchored in the bay were the *Sierra Estrella, Fiery Cross, Desdemona, Socotra, Torresdale* and the Yankee ship *Palmyra*. The names of the other ships I can't recall.

Abstracts from log of ship 'Acamas', Voyage 5; Capt. W. A. Nelson

Date	Barry Dock to Algoa Bay—	Days out
1902		
Sept. 29th	Sailed in tow tug 'Flying Cormorant', cargo coal	
Sept. 30th	Cast off tug at Lundy Island, *Departure*	
Nov. 3rd	Crossed Equator in Long. 28½ West	34
Nov. 8th	Spoke Italian S.S. 'Umbria'	
Nov. 10th	Sighted Trinidad Island, Lat. 20½ S. Long. 29 W.	41
Nov. 30th.	*Arrived Algoa Bay*	61
	Total distance sailed on passage 8,032 miles	

The five wrecks bunched together were the *Limari, Agostino, Kambo, Waimea, Hermanas*. Other ships wrecked in the same gale were the *Hans Wagner, Coriolanus, Nautilus, Sayre, Theckla, Gabrielle, Arnold, Constant, Iris, Oakworth, Emmanuel, Content*. In addition, there were the tugs *Countess Caernarvon* and *Michael Cavalieri Russo*, the steam boat *Clara* and steam lighter *Scotia*. On this occasion 63 lives and 12,500 tons of shipping were lost. The ships (as described by Basil Lubbock) were 'literally torn to pieces and piled on top of each other in the terrific surf'.

On the night of 14th November the following year another gale that swept the Cape coast accounted for the following ships, stranded at Port Elizabeth: *Arranmore, County of Pembroke, Sant' Antonia, Elda, Wayfarer, Two Brothers*. Algoa Bay, it seems, has been a graveyard for sailing ships.

Lubbock follows up the story of the *Arranmore*. She had been in collision with the S.S. *Mashona* and had gone aground.

After five months the *Arranmore* was refloated, but her fore and main masts had gone by the board, and it was found too expensive to send out masts from England, so a Dutch tug, the *Swartezee*, was sent out to the Cape, and she was successful in towing the *Arranmore* from Algoa Bay to the Clyde. This must be one of the longest tows on record, being 6,800 miles. Including time occupied in coaling the tug at Dakar, it was accomplished in 54 days, or at the rate of 130 miles a day.

The voyage of the *Swartezee* must have convinced even the most ardent supporter of sail that the days of the windjammer were nearly over.

In Algoa Bay, discharging was done into lighters alongside, and due to the adverse weather conditions the process was indeed a slow one. A strong south-east wind usually got up in the afternoons causing a nasty sea, so that the cargo lighters had to be cast off very frequently.

I noticed that nearly all the tug boats were built at Falmouth and constructed of wood, being more suitable I suppose for going alongside ships in bad weather. When I had to go ashore on business, and the weather was bad, I was transferred to the tug in a ballast-basket especially kept for the purpose, and slung from the mainyard on a burton; the tug keeping a safe distance from the ship.

It was the rule of the port for vessels to send on deck their royal and topgallant yards, also topgallant masts, to give them a better chance of riding out a gale safely at anchor. But some ships only *housed* the topgallant masts. This was all right so long as they could hold on to their anchors, but in the event of their losing or slipping the cables and attempting to beat off a lee-shore in a gale of wind, the housed topgallant masts prevented the setting of the upper topsails, thus reducing their chances of gaining the open sea.

When a considerable amount of cargo had been discharged and the *Acamas* was very light, with a lot of freeboard, we started to drag both anchors during a south-east gale. The ensign was flown from the main rigging and by the time we had drifted about a mile a very efficient tug came off to our assistance with a heavy anchor ingeniously arranged for dropping from the stern, and a long heavy rope cable coiled on the after deck.

We got the end of this cable over our bow and took a round turn on the foremast, and after it was securely hitched the tug steamed ahead and dropped the anchor. This proved effective, and we rode out the gale in safety.

But what a job we had when good weather finally came. The three anchor cables had become hitched together. For two whole days a tug held on to us while we hove short and worked from daylight to dark trying to disentangle them. A heartbreaking job, as most sailors will know from bitter experience.

We were glad to see the last of the coal cargo. Having to discharge some 3,200 tons of it ourselves was bad enough, but having to bag it and sew up the sacks gave us a lot of extra work.

After taking on about 950 tons of sand ballast we got ready to leave for Newcastle NSW, having laid at Algoa Bay since the 30th November, 1902. (On Christmas Day, in addition to the plum duff, we had omelettes made from ostrich eggs. Rather high, I thought.)

We left for Newcastle on the 19th February.

At Algoa Bay the fore and mizzen royal yards had not been sent aloft again for the passage to Newcastle, but passed down the main hatch and stowed in the 'tween-decks. This no doubt gladdened the eyes of the apprentices, who had visions of fewer buntlines to overhaul.

The ballast had been stowed with the bulk mostly in the main hatch, secured with shifting boards, and the top levelled-off and covered with two-inch deals, these in turn being tommed down from the 'tween-deck beams. The rest of the ballast was stowed aft to trim the ship a foot or so by the

Date	Algoa Bay to Newcastle N.S.W.	Days out
1903		
Feb. 19th	Left under sail in sand ballast. *Departure*	
March 4th, 5th & 6th	Strong southerly gale, ballast shifted and ship lay hove to for three days with a dangerous list	
April 3rd	*Arrived* Newcastle	43
	Total distance sailed on passage 5,707 miles	

stern. About the 4th March, when well down in the 'roaring forties', we experienced a particularly heavy gale from the south-south-east. By 6 pm sail was reduced to the three lower topsails, but in the middle watch the gale increased in intensity with a high, breaking sea. At about 2 am the ship gave a violent roll. This shifted the ballast and left us nearly on our beam ends.

At this angle the rudder had no effect on the steering. So, as the ship would neither pay off nor come to, the fore and mizzen lower-topsail sheets were let go. Just as this was done the weather main lower-topsail sheet carried away.

The din caused by these sails flogging themselves into ribbons in the gale and the clatter of the chain sheets on the steel yards was terrific. To add to the awe of the superstitious seamen, St Elmo's fire appeared on the trucks of the masts and the yard-arms, a phenomenon not uncommon in high Southern latitudes.

We managed to save the lee side of the main lower-topsail by furling the weather side and leaving it set in goose-wing fashion.

All hands were sent into the hold via the after hatch, equipped with hurricane lamps, candles and shovels to re-trim the ballast. But their efforts were not attended with much success. For every shovelful they threw to windward, two shovelfuls seemed to come back.

At daybreak two bottles of grog were passed down to the hands, as some had been on duty all night, and strange as it may seem one of these bottles went missing in transit. It was not difficult at a later stage to trace the culprit—

aged Tom Smith the wily bo'sun who, taking advantage of the semi-darkness, had buried one bottle in the sand for his future consolation.

The crew took the prank in good part, but rather suspected Paddy Doyle the mate of being an accessory, as something similar had happened before with the grog issue when all hands were working coal in Algoa Bay.

The gale continued throughout the following day, moderating only gradually. It finished on the third day in a series of squalls. All this time the ship had been lurching violently to port, the clinometer showing an extreme roll of 38 degrees, never rising to within 15 degrees of the upright, even when she rolled hard to windward.

Now, in calmer weather, steam was raised on the donkey boiler and the ballast dragged to the weather side of the hold in ballast baskets. Then water was pumped on it to make it stay put. When the ship was upright, some 60 tons of ballast were shifted in wheel-barrows to the after hatch to trim the ship more by the stern. New topsails were now bent and we set off again. For the remainder of the passage the ship behaved very well.

As we heard later, the *Senator*, one of de Wolff's ships from Liverpool, which had been at Algoa Bay and left just ahead of us, had suffered similar trouble with their ballast. They were more unfortunate, however, for the captain's wife, poor woman, who was on board with him, died during the storm. The *Senator*'s carpenter constructed a rough coffin from deals, which was caulked and pitched; and the captain had his wife's remains buried in the sand ballast. On arrival at Sydney, she was reburied at one of the cemeteries there.

I can imagine the gloom prevailing in the *Senator*'s fo'c'sle and the morbid conversation among the more superstitious of the shellbacks during the rest of the passage.

William Nelson describes his crew's fear of St Elmo's fire, and the alarm among the *Senator*'s crew at the thought of a dead woman lying in the ship's ballast. And this is not surprising. In a profession where chance played so big a part; where a thread of rope or canvas could make the difference between life and death, superstition was bound to thrive.

Even in our own supposedly enlightened times, many people indulge the notion that certain actions encourage or arrest the hand of misfortune. They avoid thirteen at table. Throw spilt salt over their shoulders. Touch wood. Avoid ladders; or seeing a new moon through the window. Tea leaves and lucky stars are counted. Signs of the Zodiac are consulted before decisions are made. Sportsmen have their mascots; their lucky and unlucky days . . . The list is almost endless.

There were many 'unlucky' things that could be done aboard ship; many 'unlucky' topics of conversation. And there still are. I have fished with old trawler skippers who forbade the mention of hares, rabbits, parsons and women while the net was down—for fear of a curse upon their catch. Small wonder that the presence of the captain's wife aboard a windjammer was the cause of head-shaking among some of the fo'c'sle shellbacks. Strangely, though, it was the captain's wife herself, poor woman, who so often had the bad luck. There are many instances of disasters at sea in which she seems to have been the only person injured or lost. In a collision between two windjammers off Cape Horn, one of the two masters, thinking his ship was on the point of going down, tried to save his wife by throwing her on board the other ship. Unfortunately he missed. Falling short, she dropped between the two hulls and was crushed to death. As it happened, neither ship sank and she was the only casualty.

On another occasion when two life-boats were being manned prior to leaving a wrecked ship, the captain—contrary to tradition—went with his wife in the first boat. He did so in order, as he thought, to save his wife, since she refused to leave without him—and the rest of the crew would not leave before she did.

The second boat survived. The first boat capsized in the surf, both the captain and his wife being drowned. It is said they were washed ashore 'still locked in each other's arms'.

Incidents such as these fostered superstition. There is no doubt that the presence of the *Senator* captain's dead wife buried in the ballast would have terrified many of the crew.

After a passage of 43 days we arrived at Newcastle NSW on the 3rd April, 1903. There we remained for more than two months, the delay being due to labour troubles in the coal industry.

The anchorage was congested with idle sailing ships. Both on the Stockton and Carrington sides of the harbour, ships lay at the ballast-jetties three and four deep. Newcastle must have more foreign soil on her native heath than any other port in the world, for ships from all quarters of the globe have deposited hundreds of thousands of tons of ballast there.

The ballast from the *Acamas* was discharged with the help of a very sagacious horse, which supplied the motive power for raising the ballast-baskets from the hold. It knew exactly how many steps were needed to raise the load high enough. It also knew the time by the ship's bell. On the sound of eight bells (noon), it would trot away for its fodder; returning at two bells (1 pm) at a much slower pace.

I think it was during our present visit that we had the thrill of watching a large four-masted barque (the *Norma*, I believe) fail to make the harbour

entrance during a heavy gale. Rolling and pitching heavily in the breaking
seas she made a remarkable sight as she dragged her anchors and got
dangerously close to the beach. Crowds of people were on the shore, expecting
her to drift on the rocks. Fortunately, the powerful local tug *Champion*
managed to connect and bring her safely to port.

On the 9th June, 1903, we left Newcastle for San Francisco, on the way
sighting Three Kings Islands, the Maitea Island (Society Group) and also
Tikehau Island. After a passage of 72 days we arrived at San Francisco.

Date	Newcastle, N.S.W. to San Francisco	Days out
1903		
June 9th	Sailed in tow, cargo coal, cast off tug. *Departure*	
June 14th	Sighted Three Kings Islands	5
July 7th	Sighted Maitea Island, Society Group	28
July 8th	Sighted Tikehau island	29
July 14th	Crossed Equator in Long. 147½ West	35
Aug. 20th	*Arrived* San Francisco	72
	Total distance sailed on passage, 8,797 miles	

There we discharged the coal for Spreckles Sugar Works, took in a small
quantity of ballast, and towed to Saucilito Bay to lay-up with many more
British ships. These included the *Helensburgh* (Captain Jefferson, of Maryport), *Lock Carron* (Captain Clarke), the *Silberhorn*, *Balmoral*, and many
others. Some ships had been there about two years.

We ran a kedge anchor out and warped the ship into shoal water until she
took the mud at low tide. The idea was to get the hull scrubbed, and painted
with white-lead and tallow as low down as possible, for a ship soon gets foul
when she remains idle.

Most of the ships were laid-up owing to the low freights offering. No British
ship would accept a freight under a guinea a ton, but the subsidised French
ships were busy loading grain for Europe, accepting 17/6 for lower hold
stowage and 10/6 for the 'tween decks; charges the Britishers could not
compete with.

Captain Alan Villiers, who discussed this voyage of the *Acamas* with
William Nelson when he met him in the 1920s, long after William's retirement, had the following comment to make:

When the well-known Maryport master, Captain W. A. Nelson, arrived at San Francisco in August, 1903, seventy-two days out from Newcastle in the ship *Acamas*, he had to lay the ship up when the coal was out, joining many more British ships. Some of them, he noted, had already been there for two years. The British ships, he said, could not accept the low rates of freight being offered—17s 6d a ton to Europe. Their minimum was 21s. But there were many subsidized French ships 'busy loading grain for Europe . . .'

The French mileage subsidy allowed them to undercut. The logical French held to their enacted view that the shipping bounties were necessary, both for ship-building and operation, as part of the defence of the country as well as of the national prosperity. Their merchant service was an adjunct to the state arsenals, helping to support men and make possible a navy. Its trained seamen formed a reserve which helped in the defence of French colonies. The Bounty Law of 1881 had useful results—for the merchant fleet of 735 vessels grossing 312,000 tons then grew in the following ten years to 1,157 ships of 520,000 tons—so they kept it.

The *Acamas* had been one in a congested harbour full of ships at Newcastle, NSW, too, all waiting to load—the big sailing ships lay there three and four deep on both the Stockton and Carrington sides of the harbour. She waited for over two months, because of labour troubles in the coal industry. She got out of San Francisco with a load of lumber from Oakland for Fremantle on a 'lump sum' basis—not a large sum, but accepted in the hope of picking up grain homeward to Europe from Australia, and so showing an eventual profit on the voyage. But there was no grain: the *Acamas* had to buy ballast, sail round to Newcastle, and wait there three months for another load of coal to San Francisco. Arrived at San Francisco, once more the ship had to lay up, reducing the crew to her apprentices, officers, sailmaker and carpenter. This sort of thing—long detentions, poor freights and far between—put many British sailing ships out of business. Most were sold for a third or a fourth of their building costs: though many were then between ten and fifteen years old and still had long lives before them.

But there was more to France's attitude towards her mercantile marine than the provision of subsidies. Her seamen were regarded as national assets and treated as such; not, like Britain's merchant sailors, as riff-raff comparable only to her 'drunken soldiery'. French seamen, moreover, had a pension fund and were assured of a place ashore. British seamen on whom the economy of the United Kingdom was totally dependent had nothing.

Desertions from British ships in 1903 were upwards of forty percent of all crews. There were fewer than seven percent from French ships. The figures speak for themselves.

As history depicts with sickening clarity, Britain's governments, of whatever persuasion, have always shown despicable meanness in the treatment of men who served their country.

Towards the end of November we took a Charter for a 'lump sum' to load a cargo of lumber at Oakland Long Wharf for Fremantle. Ballast was needed with a lumber cargo, so about 400 tons were taken and spread from the forward end of the main hatch right aft to the run, nice levelled and about four feet in depth. Had we been getting so much a standard instead of a lump sum, we would have stowed the large stones of the ballast in the limbers, under the hold flooring, in order to save space, but in this case it was not necessary.

The barque *Inverkip* lay in the opposite side of Oakland Long Wharf, and I used to visit Captain and Mrs Jones. Not long after this the *Inverkip* was rammed by the *Lock Carron* (Captain Clarke), in a most disastrous collision, when Captain Jones, his wife, and nearly all hands perished.

We sailed from Frisco on the 9th December, 1903, sighting Sunday Island 43 days out and Kings Island, Bass Strait, 60 days out. Arrived at Fremantle on the 3rd March, 1904, having been 84 days on the passage.

The four-masted ship *County of Inverness* and the *John Cooke* were our neighbours at the wharf at Fremantle, also the Swedish vessel *C. Racine*. We had hopes of getting a cargo for home, but no such luck.

Date	San Francisco to Fremantle, W. A.	Days out
1903		
Dec. 9th	Sailed in tow, cargo lumber, 400 tons ballast, and three foot deck load lumber. Cast off tug, *Departure*	
1904		
Jan. 2nd	Crossed Equator in Long. 150 48 West	24
Jan. 21st	Sighted Sunday Island	43
Feb. 16th	Sighted Kent Group Islands, Bass Strait	58
Feb. 18th	Off south end Kings Island, light head winds	60
March 3rd	*Arrived* Fremantle, Port to Port	84
	Total distance sailed on passage 9,067 miles	

The *John Cooke* had an interesting career. She was bought for £3,500 in 1909 by George Milne, who owned the *Inverness* (James Nelson's future ship). He renamed her the *Inveravon* and she sailed for Melbourne from London on Christmas Day. Not the best date for starting a voyage, some of the more superstitious might think! At any rate, it all went badly for the newly-named

Inveravon right from the start as she tried to thrash her way down-Channel against a succession of westerly gales. South of the Lizard the squalls came at her with 'hurricane force'. At length, the main topmast came down, bringing with it the mizzen royal mast and yard. Five days later, a tug picked up the drifting *Inveravon* off the Lizard Head and towed her into Falmouth, where she spent two months refitting. She eventually arrived at her port of destination 196 days out! Who knows whether any of this might have happened if she had delayed sailing until Boxing Day!

Date	Fremantle to Newcastle, N.S.W.	Days out
1904		
April 22nd	Sailed in ballast, 8 p.m. off Rottnest Island, *Departure*	
May 4th	Passed Wilsons Promontory at noon	12
May 8th	*Arrived* Newcastle	16
	Total distance sailed on passage 2,478 miles	

Again we took in ballast and sailed to Newcastle NSW, making the passage in 16 days, arriving Newcastle on the 8th May, 1904.

We found the harbour as congested as ever, with idle ships waiting their turn to load. It looked like another long spell in port.

This had been our lot at every port so far during the voyage—delays that made the voyage seem interminable, especially as none could say when and where we were likely to load for home, certainly not from Newcastle.

One of the few changes in the port since our last visit was that the Rev. Kitley had superseded the Rev. James at the Seamen's Mission. In those days the Mission thrived exceedingly, owing to the great number of seamen and apprentices at a loose end, but I fancy the good attendance was due more to straitened circumstances than religious motives. Able-seamen and senior apprentices got 5/- a week and the junior apprentices 2/6, which did not go very far for pocket money. There was a 'tailor' who supplied them with almost anything, mainly oilskins and seaboots. There was also a photographer who mainly sold pictures of the ships and group photos of the crews, some framed in model life-buoys.

The names of some of the best known nautical photographers were Temple West and Godfrey* of Newcastle, and Wilton of San Francisco.

*Godfrey, painter of the *Auchencairn*. See plate facing p. 80.

On the 3rd August we sailed for San Francisco with the usual cargo of 'black diamonds'—having been at Newcastle three months waiting for it. These were lean days for the sailing ships. What with long detentions and poor freight it is no wonder that a great many soon went out of business.

We arrived at the Farralone Islands off Frisco 74 days out and berthed the following day, the 17th October, 1904.

At San Francisco our hopes of loading for home (we had been rather optimistic on the passage) were soon dispelled on hearing the state of the freight market, and once again we joined the fleet of idle 'Limejuicers'. This time we took up our abode in Oakland Creek, putting out all the moorings we had in preparation for a long stay. The *Drummuir* and *Antiope* were our neighbours, and the *Crocodile*, Captain Wilson, arrived later.

Date	Newcastle N.S.W. to San Francisco	Days out
1904		
Aug. 3rd	Sailed in tow, cargo coal, cast off tug, *Departure*.	
Sept. 14th	Crossed Equator in Long. 148½ West	42
Oct. 16th	Sighted Farralone Islands	74
Oct. 17th	*Arrived* San Francisco, Port to Port	75
	Total distance sailed on passage 8,045 miles	

By this time our hopes of getting home seemed very remote. Of course, most of the A.B.s had cleared out with the Boarding House runners, or been paid off, leaving only the apprentices, sailmaker and carpenter to look after the ship.

I forgot to mention that during our three month stay at Newcastle, the hold had been scaled (the inside of the hull plating, that is), and painted with a mixture of fresh milk, cement and red oxide. On the discharge of the cargo we found it had kept in good condition.

About Christmas time we received the good news that the ship was to tow up the coast to Eureka and there load a full cargo of redwood for the U.K. This was the best news we had had since leaving home.

The Hammond Lumber Co. had chartered the ship and they sent their own steam schooner, the *Francis H. Leggett*, which was especially adapted for towing lumber-rafts, to tow us to Eureka. The second mate of the steam schooner came on board to act as pilot and we did some tall rolling in a heavy Pacific swell on the way.

The Eureka Bar was then considered one of the worst on the whole Pacific Coast and we had quite an exciting time entering Humboldt Bay. The channel was narrow and bordered by rocks with a heavy breaking sea and our safety depended on good steering. The pilot took his station to con the ship on top of the chart room, and two of the best helmsmen were put at the wheel. As we crossed the bar one heavy roller looked like swamping the poop, but instead it curled over amidships and washed the galley out. And this with the ship in ballast.

Once in the Bay the water was as smooth as a mill-pond and we tied up at the lumber mill on the Samoa side. By the number of visitors that came on board it appeared that this was one of the largest ships that had been to the port, though I believe the *Drummuir*, a much larger vessel, had been at Eureka some time previously.

The local people were very kind to all on board and we spent a pleasant Xmas and New Year there. The apprentices did well at the Lumber Co.'s cook-house. The old Cockney cook kept them well supplied with apples, stale doughnuts and sugar etc. A few days before we sailed, the boys were on the main topgallant yard bending the sail when, much to their disgust, they saw the cook-house destroyed by fire. This was a severe blow, for it deprived them of their promised sea-stock of good eats!

We had towed up from Frisco with a skeleton crew, and now the extra men required had arrived by coast boat from Frisco having been supplied by the Boarding House Masters at about fifty dollars per man. The bunch consisted of a Mulatto, a few Scandinavians, a Britisher and a Frenchman. Frenchy, who hailed from Brittany, was the best of all; a big cheery fellow with the bluest of blue eyes. He was a good sailor and a most cheerful shipmate; cheerful in spite of the fact that after a nine-month cruise in the Arctic he had recently been paid off an American Sealer with the princely sum of one dollar. He had signed on to share the profits of the cruise, but for a common sailor there would be no profits!

The new hands came on board in a very doped condition with few if any clothes. They all had a few plugs of chewing tobacco, blocks of sulphur matches, some cheap soap and corn-cob pipes, and that was about the lot.

On the 4th January, 1905, we sailed in tow of the steam schooner *Francis H. Leggett*, having loaded about 2,000,000 feet of redwood, all of dressed planks measuring about 14 feet x 3 feet x 7 inches and containing no knots.

On crossing the Bar there was a nasty sea running. Although it was high tide there was not too much water to spare, and when one heavy sea hit her under the bows the ship shuddered so much that we thought she had struck the bottom. However, we got safely out and when ten miles off-shore let go the tug's hawser.

This hawser, by the way, was a brand new flexible 12-inch manilla spring of the best American grade. Owing to its size it could not be secured on the bitts alone, so the end was taken to the main deck and made fast round the foremast. Our filibuster of a mate had been eyeing this rope, and when the order was given to 'let go', he took an axe and chopped it through near the fairlead—thus being left with several fathoms of hawser. This later came in handy in many ways: making sennet and rovings, and very serviceable doormats. One of these mats, made by the sailmaker of five yarn sennet and marlin hitched instead of being sewn together with twine, has been constantly in use for many years and is still in fair condition.

The start of the passage was not without incident. With a fresh quarterly wind blowing, Joe the Mulatto, who understood very little English, was the first to relieve the wheel. This almost ended in disaster. Promptly, Joe got the ship all aback and nearly took the masts out of her! Infuriated, and probably frightened, the second mate, Pete Logan, landed Joe one on the jaw and chased him forward—sending an apprentice to the wheel. The truth is that Joe was no sailor. In fact he could not do a job of any kind—and was forthwith disrated to ordinary seaman.

We soon found out that the poor fellow was crazy. Near the 'Line' one evening he jumped overboard and swam away from the ship as fast as he could, telling us that 'As you no like me I go to New York!' Anyhow, we hove-to, and after a lot of work we managed to fish him out of the water—before the sharks got him.

Poor Joe probably never realized how lucky he was. Picking someone out of the sea in emergency was never an easy matter in a sailing ship. It took many minutes to bring a windjammer up into the wind, heave her to and get a boat away. It was a case of all hands on deck. There were sheets and braces to be handled; lashings to be cut. Then the boat had to be swung out and manned. That took time. Life-boats were kept lashed down on the skids to prevent their being washed away by heavy seas. By the time a boat was under oars, Joe would have been far astern.

'After a lot of work', says William, 'we managed to fish him out . . .' And a lot of work it would have been. But it was still smart ship-handling and smart boat-handling—as *any* rescue at sea needed to be smart. William was handling the *Acamas*. Among others, his son James would have been in the boat. We can be sure of that. As James's niece said seventy years later: 'When Uncle Jim sailed with grandfather he was always given the dirty or difficult or dangerous jobs to do, for fear the crew might think he was being favoured . . .' Without doubt, James would have been the first into that boat.

Joe's usual pastime in the second dog-watch was to hide in the cowl of the forward-hold ventilator and imitate a gramophone. His voice would come booming out, intoning the Edison vocal preamble which preceded all tunes in those days. In the cold weather near the Horn he would regularly strip off his one and only shirt and spend hours washing it under the fo'c'sle head. Then he would climb up to the topgallant rigging on the foremast to hang it out to dry! But everyone was really good to this crazy fellow, and when the ship eventually paid-off, all hands subscribed towards buying him a shore-suit of clothes.

By the time we neared Cape Horn the ship had been some two-and-a-half years out of dry-dock, and this was beginning to tell on her modest sailing qualities. Even so, we sighted Cape Horn 64 days out from Eureka. A few days later, however, when carrying-on sail in a strong breeze we lost the fore topgallant mast.

We soon shaped a new mast from a spare wooden spar carried for the purpose. The spar, originally octagonal in shape, was rounded off to size in quicker time than usual because the apprentices produced a couple of fine American axes. (These, I found out later, had been stolen together with a spirit compass from the pilot-house of a laid-up 'stern-wheeler' at Eureka! At any rate, they came in very handy.)

Few ships were sighted between the Horn and the Channel, at least not sufficiently near to exchange signals. We spoke the S.S. *Commonwealth* (Lunds Blue Anchor) north of the Line, and some time later the ship *Loch Katrine*, which I fancy was now reduced to barque rig.

The wooden-legged cook of the *Loch Katrine* had an unhappy accident two years later in heavy weather on passage from Melbourne to the English Channel. A big sea pitched him off-balance against a bulkhead and his wooden leg, getting knocked out of place, went through his stomach. Neither the *Captain's Medical Guide* nor any of the Mixtures did much for him, and he 'died quietly' off the Horn.

We were delayed somewhat off the Channel by very fine weather and easterly winds. Sometimes a French fishing smack would come alongside and exchange great numbers of mackerel for salt meat and tobacco. Other visitors were numerous swallows, which rested on board and slept in our rooms while the ship was on a northerly tack, but as soon as the ship tacked to the southward they would all fly away on their northward migration.

We sighted the Old Head of Kinsale on the 19th and arrived at Queenstown on the 20th May, 1905, 136 days from Eureka. Among other vessels anchored in the Bay were the battleships *Cornwallis* and *Albermarle*.

The paddle tug *Flying Fish* was a welcome visitor when it came to tow us to Glasgow. The winds were still easterly and light and in dense fog we steered from lightship to lightship up the Irish Sea, having a narrow escape off Dublin from colliding with the Holyhead mail boat.

On arrival at Glasgow all hands were paid off. And so ended a voyage which had lasted two years and eight months.

Of the seven apprentices on board when we left England: Hemy (Phoebe), Hawes (Jack), Groom (Pompey), Robson (Robby), Stangroom (Kangy), Legras (Toby), Nelson (Agile), five completed the voyage. Legras had skinned-out in Frisco and was supposed to have got a job as a 'washer-up' in a saloon. Groom was left behind in hospital at Port Elizabeth with injuries to his back, having been knocked down the main hatch by a sling of coal, due to the ship's rolling in Algoa Bay.

Hemy and Hawes were now out of their time. Hemy got his ticket and went into steam, joining Lunds Blue Anchor Line and going third mate of the S.S. *Commonwealth*, a vessel we had signalled on the homeward passage on the unlucky 13th April. At least, *we* suffered no ill-luck, but Hemy was promoted to their new steamer *Waratah*, and so perished with the passengers and crew when she disappeared off the South African Coast. I don't know what became of Hawes.

Date	Eureka, California, to Queenstown	Days out
1905		
Jan. 4th	Sailed in tow of steam schooner 'Francis H. Leggett', cast off tug, 10 miles off shore. *Departure*	
Jan. 31st	Crossed Equator (Pacific) in Long. 114 West	27
March 10th	Passed Cape Horn, strong S.W. gale	65
April 10th	Crossed Equator (Atlantic) in Long. 27 West	96
April 13th	Spoke S.S. 'Commonwealth', Lunds Blue Anchor Line	
May 1st	Spoke barque 'Loch Katrine', Melbourne to U.K., 86 days.	
May 19th	Off Old Head of Kinsale, Light East winds	135
May 20th	*Arrived* Queenstown, passage port to port	136
	Total distance sailed on passage 15,975 miles	

This passage was rather a long one but as the ship was foul, not having been in dry dock since July 1902 at Rotterdam, it might have been much worse.

The tug 'Flying Fish' towed ship to Glasgow where the cargo of Red-wood was discharged.

VOYAGE 6

From Glasgow the ship went in tow to Port Talbot to load coal for Pisagua on the West Coast of Chile. This voyage, I had firmly made up my mind, would be my last. Most last voyages are not attended with much success—and this one was no exception.

There is no question that, if only for weather alone, this was to be William's worst voyage. And it is a tribute to his seamanship that the *Acamas* not only survived the passage westwards round Cape Horn but achieved it in the time she did.

This voyage, the sixth of the *Acamas*, is notable, too, for a new addition to the ranks of the apprentices on board: Thomas Brabban Marsham, James Nelson's lifelong friend, had joined the ship at Glasgow.

All went well until we had just got through the Straits of Le Maire near Cape Horn. Standing to the southward under topsails in snow blizzards and a westerly gale, we were suddenly caught aback by a terrific squall from the S.S.W. Although the upper-topsail halyards were let go, the yards failed to come down owing to the pressure of the sails against the masts and the heavy list we had taken before gathering sternway. Fortunately we got round on the same tack again without getting dismasted—but it must have been a very near thing.

After that it blew so hard, with fierce snow and hail squalls, that we were forced to find shelter under Staten Island. There we remained for a few days, in company with one of Walmsley's barques, the *Lorton*, I think.

It was now towards the end of September 1905 and the Cape Horn weather seemed to be at its worst, very cold, and the gales ever from the Westward. We spent from two to three weeks off the pitch of the Horn, most of the time in company with the four-masted French ship *Tarapaca*, both ships always going about together on the various tacks. On one tack we got to nearly sixty degrees South trying to get a slant of wind.

One morning as we head-reached against the gale, we found the ship was down by the head and making heavy weather by shipping more water than usual forward. The force-pump pipe had got fractured in the fore peak—which had filled with water to sea level. It was fortunate that this break came when it did, and that we had the peak baled out and the fracture repaired with canvas and white lead, before the weather turned really bad.

About ten days later, just before dark, both the *Acamas* and the *Tarapaca* wore ship to the northward. While we were doing so the wind came away from the S.W. with hurricane force. The sea was mountainous, with a cross N.W. swell. The last we saw of the *Tarapaca* she was running across our bows in the twilight during a hail squall. She was rather too close for comfort, we thought, but she looked a wonderful sight as she sped before the gale under close-reefed topsails.

We ran to the northward all night all hands in the poop ready for any emergency. We had barely got in sufficient 'westing' so had to keep the wind well out on the port quarter. The two best helmsmen were kept at the wheel, getting a small tot of rum periodically to warm them.

A tub filled with straw was kept near the wheel in ordinary Cape Horn weather for the helmsman to stand in and keep his feet from being frost bitten,* but that went missing on this terrible night as the ship pooped once or twice and everything moveable had been washed away. A high dangerous sea swept the main deck throughout the night as the ship staggered along about 12 knots under lower topsails.

When daylight came it revealed something of a mess. The weather door of the half-deck had been stove-in. The partition bulkhead in the thwartship alleyway dividing the apprentices' room from the P.O.s' had come down bringing with it the bunks attached. There were some two feet of water in the room surging from side to side, the bunk boards were smashed to match-wood as they washed about. Sea chests, underclothes, tins of stockholm tar and tallow (for seaboots), hardtack—now soft—mingled with swollen plugs of tobacco, the remains of donkey's breakfasts (straw mattresses), well seasoned enamelled cups (the colour of mahogany inside from the tannin deposit from our crew tea) all these and sundry other articles formed a flotsam scarcely worth salvaging.

Our next discovery was more alarming. The main hatch had been stove-in, the steel strong-back having snapped in half. Fortunately, the hatches had dropped down on the coal cargo instead of going overboard. The tarpaulins were in shreds, although still held in the cleats. A great deal of water must have gone down into the hold during the night. We also found the starboard bulwarks abreast of the main hatch had been bent outboard and several stanchions torn away from the waterways. The rivets had dropped out of the holes into the hold as the decks constantly flooded.

It was still blowing hard, with the decks awash, so the ship was hove-to. 'Chips' made a number of wooden plugs, after which a couple of the apprentices went into the hold, climbed over the coal and drove these plugs into the vacant rivet holes.

The big job was to secure the main hatch. But where to find the material to do it with? A sailing ship deep-loaded off the Horn has very little spare timber about the decks. Although all hands were by now very tired, there was no alternative but to send them down into No. 1. 'tween decks and to drag out as many 'shifting boards' as they could get. These boards were long 2 inch deals, lashed with rope yarns in a fore-and-aft direction to the line of midship stanchions. It was no easy matter getting these out as they were buried in coal with only the forward ends of the planks exposed. The men, numbed with the cold, were dressed in oilskins with soul and body lashings.

Coal had to be shifted until the ropeyarn lashings holding the planks to the stanchions could be cut. And even after that, they took a lot of dragging out. However, by 4 pm there were sufficient planks available. But to get these along the deck was another job, as occasional heavy seas kept tumbling on

---

*This idea may have come from the local Cumbrian miners who used to put straw in their clogs at night, ready for the morning; the air in the straw being a fine insulator.

board. So, a length of small rope was attached to the ends of each plank and secured to the belaying pins on the ship's rail whenever the sea came along.

By 5 p.m. we had the hatch covered with deals, lashed securely down to the ring-bolts in the hatch coamings, and before dark a new storm sail was spread over the lot and well lashed round the coamings. One watch was now sent below. The other watch got coal up to raise steam on the donkey. They also rigged the messenger chain from the winch to the main pumps as it was necessary to get the pumps working as soon as possible. There was about eight feet of water in the wells.

Fortunately, this was the last gale Cape Horn had in store for us. The wind gradually moderated to a fresh Southerly, and we soon got into fine, warm weather, where we could spread out our mildewed clothes in the sun for an airing.

Sailing into Pisagua Bay with a European pilot on board we faced another mishap. Baffling winds were met with and he gave orders to let go the anchor. This was done, but the brakes on the windlass failed to check the cable, which ran out at great speed—with the resultant loss of our anchor and 135 fathoms of chain. This was a serious matter as it meant waiting to get another from England.

We had made the passage out in 109 days, the longest passage I ever made to the West Coast. All the same, it was not so bad, comparatively speaking. Some of the ships which left about the same time as us took about 130 days or longer. I fancy two of these ships were the *Ladye Doris* and the *British Isles*.

The French barque *Anne* arrived at Pisagua in 135 days, having sailed East About round the Cape of Good Hope and south of New Zealand. But the French ships got paid so much for every mile they sailed as a subsidy from their Government, therefore distance was no object.

Arriving at Pisagua in early November, we were destined to remain there until the following May. Needless to say, we didn't suspect this at the time. Had such a dreadful prospect been presented to us on our arrival we might all have gone demented. For the sailor, this port was the world's worst!

When one considers the dangers and hardship of the sea, it might be thought that to navigate a windjammer in safety halfway round the world was sufficiently testing; that on reaching harbour, no skipper could do other than breathe a sigh of relief. But in truth many a harrassed commander must sometimes have envied his ghostly counterpart aboard *The Flying Dutchman*— the ship that sails for ever and never reaches port—for so often it was not until his ship had berthed that a master's troubles really started.

William's pet aversion seems to have been Pisagua: the worst port in the world, he called it. And perhaps it was. But according to these letters sent to the ship's owners by Captain D. B. Shaw of the American barque *Saranack*, Fremantle must have run it pretty close!

FREMANTLE
October 27, 1892

Messrs Simpson & Shaw
NEW YORK

Gentlemen,

I arrived here Oct. 21st p.m. 22nd being Saturday and a short day done nothing. Sunday done nothing. 24th Entered and fought against putting the vessel alongside the Jetty to discharge. It is a terrible place. No place to put a vessel, no shelter whatever. All the ships have to lay discharging at the wharf or pay lighterage. I began this morning. Got out about 50 Tons. Have to hoist with an engine. Can't do without one. Have to pay 50/- per day for that. Captain Shaw told me that this was a very cheap port. It is not so. It is a very expensive port and the worst I was ever in.

This loading for two ports in one ship is a mistake and a great big one. Nearly half of the cargo in tween decks so far is Launceston cargo and it has to be handled over so many times to make room. My crew are half drunk. Some of them have cleared out and the others too drunk to work. I am afraid that there won't be a great big dinner left off the Fremantle freight. I have not received any letters or papers from you. Hope you are so busy in the Store that you could not find time to write.

I am, Gentlemen,
   Your obedient Servant,
     D. B. Shaw

FREMANTLE
November 8th, 1892

Messrs Simpson & Shaw
NEW YORK

Gentlemen,

I am having very hard luck in getting discharged. The weather has been very bad ever since I arrived and tonight it is blowing a gale of wind from the S.W. With a S.W. wind the water keeps pretty smooth but the spray is flying all over the ship. My lines are all used up and I have got two heavy springs hired to make her fast aft, and out ahead I have my anchors down with 75 fathoms of chain out and all the remaining lines that I have left and one of my bow chains fast to the wharf and it takes all our time to hold her. Once in a while there is a terrible run comes in. Then I have to slack her off and let her go. It is impossible to hold her. She would tear herself all to pieces. She has done considerable damage to herself. My after bits are broken off level with the deck. My stern chocks are pulled out and about 10 feet of the rail all torn off including two stanchions. All of my channels next to the dock are more or less damaged. About 8 feet of my main rail is split off and one hawse pipe gone. The bufalow on the starboard side of the top-gallant forecastle all twisted up. Don't believe I can fix it without changing it. My lines are all ruined. It is certainly the worst place I or anyone else ever saw. No place to send a ship of this size. If I get clear without any more damage I will be in luck. She is turning out her cargo in grand order but it is all mixed up. There is almost as much Launceston cargo in the tween decks as there is Fremantle and it makes slow work discharging, the cargo has to be handled over so many times. The tween decks and the fore-hold are all out. Tomorrow is a Government holiday. No work. Can't work in the hold. Everything sealed up. I have an engine hoisting. Can't do without. The wharf is high and the cargo has to be landed into railway trucks. Five of my crew have run away and one is sick, so you see I have not too many to work cargo. Have to hire considerable labour. I don't know what I will do for sailors. Everyone goes to the gold diggings and wages are £5 per month. It will take me two days to restow my Launceston cargo. The greater part of the heavy stuff will have to go into the lower hold. I am afraid that she will have none too much cargo for ballast.

I hope to get away this week if the weather gets fine. It is a mistake loading cargo for two ports, nothing in it but expense and loss of time. I met with a curious accident the other day. The ship was rolling about and a sling load of cargo capsized into the dock. Three of the cases were cartridges and one beef. I got a Diver to go down. He got two cases of cartridges. Said he could not find any more. I had to pay him £2. The cartridges were worth about £25. It was too bad but it was not through carelessness. I would not come to this port again if they made me a present of the vessel. I never get any rest day or night. Keeps me all the time running fixing something up. Fenders grind up as fast as I put them in. I have bought two sets besides the one I had on board.

I remain, Gentlemen,
  your Obedient Servant,
    D. B. Shaw

                                                              FREMANTLE
                                                         November 11, 1892

Gentlemen:
  You will please find enclosed the First of Exchange for £500. I hope to get finished discharging today. I have been two days shifting cargo trying to find 5 cases of machine oil.

When I left the ship they had found 5 cases stowed under the Launceston cargo in the lower hold. It has been the devil's own job. It is now blowing heavy from the S.W. and may last two or three days. Can't get clear of the wharf until it moderates. No steam power than can tow her. It is a bad job coming here. I will remit you balance when I get settled up. The vessel is 6 feet by the stern and I have hoisted nearly all the cargo out of the after hold and run it forward. It will take some few days to restow the cargo and retrim the ship before I can go to sea. Will get away as soon as possible.

I am, Gentlemen,
   Your Obedient Servant
      D. B. Shaw

FREMANTLE
November 18th, 1892

Gentlemen,
   It is now 8 days since I finished discharging at the Pier and I have been ever since trying to get settled up but I have not got wound up yet. I hope to-day. We cannot find all the cargo. We have broken out and restowed nearly all the lower hold and have found a great many packages mixed up with the Launceston cargo. There is a lot of cargo that is windmills packed in crates. The stevedores knocked them to pieces in order to make good stowage. By doing so the mark and number is lost and there is no telling who it belongs to. It doesn't matter how small a thing is wanted to make the lots complete. They put in a claim for the most expensive things they can and when I have to go to the Warehouse and open everything and find out what is wanted. I have found all but a bundle of pump rods, 5 cans of Beef, 9 cans of Kerosene. The Beef I can't find and will have to pay for it. The Oil I won't pay for as it was tallied out of the ship alright. The bill for the pump rods they have billed me for 75 dollars and the whole pump only cost 28 dollars in New York. I am in hopes of getting the matter fixed up before noon. The consignees started in with Claims for short-delivery amounting to £700. I have got it all down to £25.
   Gentlemen I have been in a good many places in my time but this is the worst damned hole I ever saw. No one will do anything but work against the ship. There was one man sent in a claim for £4 for shortage of a case of tinned fruit. The case went out alright. I refused to pay it and they summoned me to Court and I had to pay. Things would go much better if the ship landed all her cargo here. A Mate's tally is no good in the Court. They only acknowledge the Wharf Tally and they are half drunk all the time and don't care what they do. The ship has to feed them and give them all the money and tobacco they want or they will make trouble. They are a dirty lot. I am in hopes of getting finished up so I can mail the balance of freight to-day but I'm afraid I won't. I came on shore two days ago with the boat. It began to blow. The boat could not get off and they are ashore yet. It is blowing a gail from the N.W. Can't get a tug boat or anything else to put them on board. They refused to receive the cartridges that went

overboard and I have got to take them away with me. Will try to sell them in Launceston. They are all good that I have tried but they have been wet and the paper boxes they are packed in have all tumbled to pieces.

I am, Gentlemen,
  Your Obedient Servant
    D. B. Shaw

FREMANTLE
November 19th, 1892

Messrs Simpson & Shaw
NEW YORK

Gentlemen,
  You will please find enclosed a Draft on London for £200. There is about £58 in Merchant's hands yet which they won't pay until the balance of claims are paid which won't be today. I was never so sick of a place in my life and may the curse of Christ rest on Fremantle and every son of a bitch in it. God damn them all.

I remain Gentlemen,
  Your Obedient Servant
    D. B. Shaw

P.S. Any man that would come or send a ship a second time is a damned ass. The mail closes at 1 p.m today sharp and the Bank wont give me a draft until 1 p.m. so it wont get away by this mail. It is some of the Agent's doings I think but do not know for sure. Still blowing a heavy gale.

  D.B.S.

At Pisagua, little better off than Captain Shaw, William found himself faced with some 3,200 tons of dusty Welsh coal to be sewn up in sacks and discharged into lighters.

A dirty back-breaking job. And at the end of the day's work, only a limited ration of fresh water was available for washing, as fresh water was almost unobtainable and very expensive. As it never seems to rain in this part of the world, there was no rainwater to get.

Fresh meat and vegetables were just as scarce. About every ten days a coast boat would arrive with a few head of cattle to serve local requirements and if one was not at the market very soon after the beasts were killed the chances of getting meat were very slight. The cattle were slaughtered on a small wooden wharf on the water front, and the apprentice going ashore in the boat for the meat would watch until the cattle had been cut up and then hurry to put in his order: 65 lb a two-days' supply. It was no use getting more, as it would not keep long in the hot climate. For vegetables, the ship's boat would be sent off to meet the coast-boat, and as soon as she anchored these would be purchased direct. At other times we got them in small quantities from the local market.

Fish were scarce, or at least difficult to catch! The only way we succeeded in catching any was by blowing them up with cigarette tins containing small charges of dynamite. I and Captain Lever of the ship *Imberhorne* took the ship's boat on one of these expeditions. In shallow water we threw out food to get the fish together, lighted the fuses with our cigars, then threw the tins overboard. After the explosion a dozen or so small flat-fish came to the surface, stunned and swimming on their backs. These were netted and put in the boat. But the result of an afternoon's dynamiting was somewhat disappointing.

Another day we equipped the *Imberhorne*'s boat with sails and refreshments. Captain Lever brought his young daughters with him, and rowed by the apprentices we proceeded to Junin, the next port to the southward, to visit our friend Captain Mackenzie of the barque *Lota*.

Previous to the *Lota*, Captain Mackenzie had commanded the bald-headed barque *Nithsdale*; later sold to the Germans and renamed *Cape Horn*.

No wind came throughout the day, so the apprentices had a long pull both ways. We had expected to pull all the way outward and to sail back with a fair wind when the afternoon breeze made. But the boys were used to long pulls.

It was the practice that whenever a ship sailed homeward, the captains of the other ships in port would go on board and their boat crews give a hand in heaving up the anchor, loosing and setting sail. The boats would be towed astern until the homeward-bounder was five or six miles off-shore, then the half-dozen or so ship's boats would have a race back to their various ships, which meant a lot of hard pulling.

One day aboard the *Acamas*, a sling of sacks of coal fell on a 'launchero' (or lighterman) and broke his leg. This accident let us in for all kinds of trouble. The lighterman happened to be a Peruvian, so I saw the Peruvian Consul and we interviewed the injured man in hospital and settled a fair sum by agreement for compensation. But when the Captain of the Port found out what we had done he was furious, as he himself had got nothing out of it. In revenge, a few days later, while I was ashore he sent the police boat off to the ship to bring the mate to him under arrest. The mate was thrown in prison among a lot of criminals with ball-and-chain on their feet. His diet consisted of brown beans.

On seeing the British Consul I was informed that the Judge would release the mate only on the sum of 500 Pesos being paid. The mate was charged with 'culpable negligence'; and as the charge was against the mate and not the ship it rather complicated matters, because the mate hadn't 500 Pesos in the world.

The British Consul was of no help and showed little interest until I wrote to the British Minister at Santiago explaining that unless the mate was released the ship would be detained indefinitely, as the second mate had no certificate, the proper second mate having previously been paid-off and sent home sick.

In the end the Agents paid over the fine and the mate was released. But how he got on in settling with the owners after arriving home, I never knew.

One night all hands were awakened by a heavy rumbling noise and the ship shaking. Most of us thought for a moment that the ship had drifted ashore on the rocks. But it turned out to be an earthquake. This did some slight damage to the town. One of our A.B.s who was in hospital with a broken leg said all the lights went out, and everyone that could move ran out of the hospital at once, leaving the helpless to shift for themselves.

We had been waiting for a new anchor and cable to be sent, and by the time these arrived on the S.S. *Lord Derby* we had taken in a part cargo of nitrate and were nearly ready to sail for Antofagasta to complete the loading. By this time we were rather short-handed as some of the sailors had cleared out and were supposed to be working at the saltpetre mines. One or two others who had been given leave ashore were serving in gaol for getting drunk. It was the practice to give the sailors a day's liberty on the West Coast, and this invariably meant a bad time for a few of them.

The first thing they did on getting ashore was to get in the nearest saloon and fill themselves with 'fire-water'. The police well knew their failing and would watch for them. A mounted gendarme, whenever he saw a drunken sailor, would lassoo his victim and drag him off to the Calaboose. There he was stripped of everything he had and put into the chain gang, and for several days this gang would be employed in cleaning the streets under guard. Other sailors would get into quarrels with the Chilanos and often end up by being severely stabbed, the Chilano being an expert with the knife which he always carried.

There were no seamen available in Pisagua, so it was arranged that we would sail with the few we had—the wages of the men short to be shared among the crew present. It meant of course that all hands had to be prepared to turn out at any time of day or night to assist the few on watch.

Antofagasta was only about 240 miles to the southward of Pisagua. But to sail there was another matter, because the prevailing wind is permanently from the South and the tidal current always running North, which made it impossible to beat to windward. Even if there had been a tug available, the cost would in all probability have been prohibitive. To get to Antofagasta we *had* to sail there and it seemed to me there was only one way of doing it.

At any rate we got underway and stood out on the port tack, on the same track that homeward-bound ships sailed towards the Horn. We kept on this port tack until we ran out of the southern limits of the S.E. trade wind, in about Lat. 30 degrees South. Then we sailed in towards the coast with the westerly wind and, after making a landfall, coasted to the northward with the southerly breeze until we reached Antofagasta—making double sure not to over-run our port, otherwise the passage would have had to be done all over again!

This coastal trip took about 18 days, sailing about 2,000 miles to reach a port a little over 200 miles away!

Yes, but a smart bit of sailing. How important it was that William made his landfall *south* of Antofagasta and, having done so, took care not to get swept past the port by the strong-flowing northerly tidal current—otherwise, as he said, he would have had to sail those two thousand miles all over again!

Incoming ships, sailing from the Horn to one of the southern ports on the South American West Coast, and lacking a breeze to take them into harbour, had been known to drift helplessly past, northwards—if no tug happened to be available at the right moment! Unable to beat back against the current, the frustrated skippers who, up to then, may have made exemplary passages, found themselves faced with no alternative to making huge detours—similar to that sailed by the *Acamas* when making good her two hundred and forty miles south from Pisagua to Antofagasta.

At Antofagasta we moored near the ship *Dalgonar* (Captain Isbester, an old friend of mine). Another ship there was the *Scottish Hills and Lochs*, having a long stay in the port and being used by the German Cosmos Line for storing their cargoes during local labour troubles. I believe that many a tinned plum-pudding was 'discovered' by the *Scottish Hills and Lochs'* apprentices while their vessel was a store-ship!

About July, 1906, the *Acamas* and the *Dalgonar* sailed from Antofagasta for Rotterdam. We sighted the *Dalgonar* only once on the passage, making the Horn in misty rain, and beat her to Rotterdam by at least a week.

During November, 1906, the *Acamas* towed over to London, there to load a general cargo for Melbourne. To me this seemed rather tantalizing, because during my continuous 44 years at sea, although I had been many times to Australia I had never had the good fortune to visit Melbourne. And now that I was leaving to go into retirement the ship heads for that very place!

Captain Bright relieved me, but the *Acamas* only made another voyage or two under the British flag. After this she was sold to the Norwegians and renamed *Gezina*. She went missing on a voyage from Rio Janeiro to New York in 1918.

16

The *Ladas*

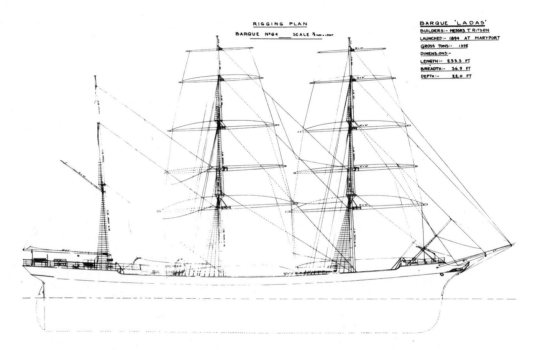

RIGGING PLAN

BARQUE N°64   SCALE ⅛ INCH = 1 FOOT

BARQUE 'LADAS'
BUILDERS:- MESSRS T RITSON
LAUNCHED:- 1894 AT MARYPORT
GROSS TONS:- 1395
DIMENSIONS:-
LENGTH:- 233.3 FT
BREADTH:- 36.9 FT
DEPTH:- 22.0 FT

I had been ashore in retirement about nine months when Mr Ritson asked me if I would like to make another voyage. He wanted a master for his barque *Ladas*.

The vessel was then loading a general cargo in Salthouse Dock, Liverpool, and bound to Callao—having been chartered by Messrs Walmsley for a lump sum.

A nice story is told about the *Ladas* in Salthouse Dock by William's daughter, Margaret. 'We were lying in the dock at Liverpool and there was a steamer berthed ahead of us. She was flying the Blue Peter, and when the hawsers were cast off someone gave the order "Full speed astern"—and she ran backwards into Father's ship. He was furious, leapt off the *Ladas* and ran all the way round the dock to get the dock gate closed to prevent the steamer getting away.'

The *Ladas* was a weatherly little craft, but rather a poor sailer with the wind aft. One story has it that she once found herself embayed with icebergs, and that only her good qualities of sailing to windward saved her from destruction.

This is true. Captain Alfred Hodgson of Maryport who sailed in the *Ladas* on several of her early voyages has given an account of it.

I had heard of Capt. Pattman sailing the *Loch Torridon* some fifty miles through huge bergs, as he supposed, only to find that he was embayed in an ice island, and had difficulty in beating his way out again, and I can well believe it in view of our experience in the *Ladas*.

We had sailed about 40 miles along the south side of a great mass of ice, and it stretched as far as we could see to the south and east, with no sign of a break. Many anxious nights we passed, especially when the wind freshened from the westward and the white horses began to curl, as it was very difficult on a dark night to distinguish ice from foam.

One never-to-be-forgotten night we were bowling along under main topgallant sail, wind strong west. About 9 o'clock, ice was reported by the look-out on the port bow. About 10 o'clock it was reported on the starboard bow, and soon afterwards right ahead! We then discovered we were sailing into a large bay of ice. Quick action was necessary.

To clew up the main topgallant, and brace the yards sharp up on the starboard tack was only the work of a few minutes, and here is where the *Ladas* showed her good weatherly qualities. She stood up to it grandly.

None but those who have experienced a trying ordeal such as this can adequately understand it. Death indeed was very near. There was no hope at all should anything go amiss, or any gear part. We had little to spare when at last we cleared the S.W. horn of the berg. The all-important question was, how far the ice might extend under the water? We had several near shaves before we were able to square away again, as we had to weather the N.W. corner before we were able to keep the *Ladas* on her course.

This was only one of many anxious nights and days. Most of the bergs we passed were from 500 to 1,000 feet long, and from 40 to 150 feet high. Some took on very fantastic shapes, appearing like castles, or churches with steeples.

Captain Hodgson also told a good story about a race between the *Ladas* and two American windjammers, which shows how fast she must have been to windward.

With the wind abaft she was very ordinary, but with it abeam she could hold her own with almost anything that came along, in fact I never saw anything pass her nor weather her when she had the wind abeam.

Captain Tom Messenger commanded her on her maiden voyage, but about 1896 he left the ship at Liverpool and Captain Robert Dixon, another fine Maryport master, took over command. We loaded cargo in the West Waterloo Dock and sailed in May 1896 for Honolulu, Sandwich Islands.

Captain Dixon had a thorough knowledge of Cape Horn weather and took the *Ladas* round in fine style. Seeming to sense every move in the game, he did some hard driving in the face of head winds and got round without trouble.

At Honolulu, on working out of the port, two of Sprekel's vessels passed us bound for 'Frisco, as we were. They hailed us in passing saying they would report us when they got to 'Frisco. On getting outside we saw them beating through the passage between Oahu and Molokai, but as we were in ballast we kept round to the westward of Oahu. We arrived in 'Frisco on a Sunday and the following Tuesday the first of the Sprekel vessels arrived, the *W. G. Irving*. Her skipper had the biggest surprise of his life when he found we were ahead of him. I was in Balfour Williamson's office with Captain Dixon when the Yankee came bowling in. His first remark was: 'Where is that Britisher? I never thought to live to see the day that a—Limey would show me the way from Honolulu to 'Frisco!'

A story that nicely illustrates not only the speed of the *Ladas* to windward, but the professional rivalry between windjammer skippers. Now to return to the *Ladas* under William Nelson.

We sailed in August, 1907, for Callao, loaded down to our marks, with a crew consisting mainly of aliens. The first mate was old and experienced, but rather eccentric; the second mate had no certificate. By now, sailing vessels were finding it difficult to get remunerative cargoes. In consequence, their upkeep was being neglected and the low wages paid to crews were no inducement for good men to sign-on.

On towing down the River Mersey with the ebb tide it soon became apparent that my very 'last' voyage was not going to be attended with much success. As we were about to pass the Formby Lightship there was a grave misunderstanding between the tug-master and our pilot. The tug passed on one side of the lightship whereas our pilot had altered course to pass on the other!

So close were we to the lightship that it was hopeless for me to have countermanded the pilot's order to the helmsman. With the strong ebb tide running there would certainly have been a collision if I had. Just in time the tug slipped his hawser—and to save the ship from grounding we let go both anchors. Unfortunately, what with the strong tide and our having too much headway, both anchors and cables were lost.

Well, much better that than losing the ship. But pretty desperate stuff just the same. It all reads as if the pilot was drunk—although we can be sure that he wasn't. William's daughter, Margaret, remembers a pilot boarding the *Acamas* the worse for drink. 'Father would not let him take the ship in.'

No, the incident was simply, as he says: 'A grave misunderstanding.' But what a misunderstanding! We can picture the scene. The lightship—straining at her mooring-chains with the ebb tide piled against her bows—looming up with frightening swiftness. Aboard the tug, a cat-like leap to the cable quick-release. Aboard the *Ladas* a bang of sledge-hammers as the mates knock away the anchor wedges—the roar of her cables through the hawse-pipes as she surges on with the tide under her . . . Then, suddenly, with a jolt that nearly jerks out the ship's masts and a noise like cannon-shots, the cable ends part at the shackles . . .

We may imagine the flow of obscenity aboard the tug. But not, perhaps, aboard the *Ladas*. 'Grandfather', says his granddaughter, Christine, 'was very religious. You may recall that in one ship he was the only person to have a prayer-book [shades of his covenanting ancestors]. He did not approve of swearing.'

The tug then came and took us in tow again and brought us back to Birkenhead where we intended to wait for new anchors and chains. But our ill-luck still stuck to us. On entering the docks at Birkenhead we collided with the quay wall, carrying away the bobstay and doing damage to our bowsprit.

After a stay of ten days or so we sailed again. This time we got safely away out of the river and the Channel, and all went well for a few weeks until the first mate suddenly went out of his mind and had to be kept locked up in his cabin. This was a serious matter for all concerned, for not only was there the extra work and anxiety of looking after him, but it meant that I was the only competent navigator left, with no experienced watch-keeper to take charge on deck while I was below.

I decided to put back to Monte Video and there land the mate and get another in his place. But ill-luck still prevailed. On reaching across the entrance of the River Plate towards Monte Video in fine clear weather, with cross-bearings showing the ship in the fairway, she struck some submerged obstruction and began to leak. This meant that on our arrival at Monte Video the cargo had to be discharged into a hulk so that repairs could be made to the ship's hull. During all this the cargo suffered a great deal from pilferage and rough handling. It was typical of the voyage. Nothing it seemed could go right.

After a very long spell in Monte Video, repairs were finally made, the cargo was reloaded and we sailed again with a new first mate.

Off Cape Horn we got a severe 'dusting' in a long series of westerly gales, but finally arrived 'all well' at Callao.

From Callao we proceeded to Taltal and loaded nitrate for Antwerp, making an average and uneventful passage home.

At Antwerp the ship was laid up and with my family I lived on board for nine months—when the ship was sold to the Norwegians.

And so came to an end my last voyage to sea, and with it a seafaring career of 47 years in sail—of which, 36 were spent in command.

On arrival in Antwerp docks, then surrounded by marshland, William's daughter Margaret, who was aboard with her mother, was greeted by the captain of the ship lying alongside.

'Be very careful,' he said. 'The mosquitoes are as big as camels!'

So, in 1909, William Andrew Nelson comes ashore for good. In all conscience, forty-seven years in one of the most demanding jobs on earth is long enough. And seventy is a fair age. Even so, I have a feeling that it was the rapidly approaching eclipse of sail rather than any weakening of his faculties that brought about the final retirement. After all, he had just sailed the *Ladas* unscathed through a 'severe dusting' off Cape Horn. Physically, he was still as sound as a rock. But the worsening crews for sailing ships, and skeleton crews at that; the difficulty of getting cargoes; the long periods of forced inactivity in foreign ports, had become intensely depressing. The last voyage of the *Acamas*, dragging out with those dreary months rotting in Pisagua, had drained his enthusiasm. At last, the sea had lost its relish. The *Ladas* had been taken on her final voyage under the Ritson house flag simply to oblige an old friend. He knew that sail was finished.

In 1891 there had been 10,918 sailing ships (tonnage 2,827,822) registered in the United Kingdom, manned by crews numbering 80,124. By 1910, the year after William's retirement, the number of ships had decreased to 4,967, the tonnage to 890,172, and the crews to 25,628. By comparison, the number of steamers had increased from 6,122 in 1891 to 9,421 in 1910; the tonnage from 5,316,808 to 10,409,196, and the crews from 159,232 to 250,428.

But William Nelson had no wish to serve in steam. He was a sailing man through and through. His professional record rests not on a heap of coal, but wind and rope and canvas.

It all takes shape as one reads back through the log books. Never a shipwreck. Just the one stranding, off Spilsby Island (when the bearing compass had been tampered with) and he sailed the ship off unaided, anyway. Three men lost overboard in thirty-six years of command. Some ships lost that number with a single wave of Cape Horn. Never an apprentice lost—that most vulnerable of all hands that ever went to sea in sail. And he seems never to have made a bad landfall. Add to that his list of consistently fast passages and you have a seafaring record that few captains can have equalled.

'He was a *satisfying* master to serve with,' it was said of him. 'All his ships were satisfying ships.'

It is true. And the proof is there in the logs.

But when reviewing his career what impresses me most about this astonishing man, even above his standard of seamanship and navigation, is his physical fitness. One expects toughness from a seaman of that era; indeed, had he not been hardy, William—who was only a youngster at the time—would scarcely have survived that horrible voyage in the *James Jardine*. But it is the absence of any sort of illness that is so remarkable. Except for the attack of fever at Calcutta in 1862, and the cold he caught during his first 'retirement' in 1907, he seems never to have ailed during the whole of his life.

But for all his toughness and the strictness of his shipboard discipline, there was a tender side. His granddaughter, Christine Dixon, says of him: 'He loved children. When we were all staying at Ivegil, the home of Captain Tom Scott who at one time commanded the *Ladas*, my cousin Eric came out in spots through eating too many green apples. Grandfather was delighted. Believing that Eric had caught measles, he thought his grandchildren would have to be kept there in quarantine and unable to go home at the end of the holidays!'

His daughter Margaret remembers that while she was a student in Edinburgh—William believed in his daughters being trained to earn their own living, if necessary—she once got an extended holiday when visiting the *Ladas* in Antwerp in 1909. William decided the weather was too bad for her to return. On another occasion, when she was very young, she was the only Nelson child not seasick on a very rough passage to Rotterdam. Delighted, William bought her a pair of leather boots.

They were pretty tough themselves, those Nelson children. 'I remember once when we were all aboard the *Acamas* in the River Elbe,' says Margaret.

Those parts of William Nelson's memoirs that were not written down by one of his daughters during visits to his ship at the completion of a voyage, were scribbled on spare pages of his Abstract Logs. He made repeated attempts to get started, re-working the first page or two over and over again—as though searching for a literary style. Under the heading: 'Some memories of my seafaring life', here is one version, written in an old *Ladas* logbook when he was 86.

'My brother James took Jane and me out on the painter's raft, which was moored alongside. We had a wonderful time going up and down on the swell made by the wakes of the ships going up to Hamburg. The captain of one of these ships later came on board to lunch and said to our parents: "And do you know, there was a raft with three children on it, bobbing up and down in the wake of the ships . . . They might all have been drowned.'

'We kept very straight faces. But Father must have guessed who it was. I think secretly he was quite proud of us.

'It was exciting when we met the ship and joined Father off Queenstown or in the Channel. We would climb aboard up the rope ladder the pilots used, or get swung up in a bo'sun's chair.

'I think it was in Rotterdam after Father's last voyage in the *Acamas*, when the apprentices tried to smuggle a box of chocolates into the girls' cabin by means of a rope to the porthole—but it was fielded by Mother in the cabin next door. She would give us one chocolate each, after dinner.

'Early one morning Jane and I rowed across the harbour, but at the harbour steps Jane slipped and fell in . . . To try to hide this piece of bad seamanship from Father, Jane was smuggled into the galley to dry while I went and fetched her some clean clothes. But she couldn't get her hair dry in time for breakfast, so put it in plaits. Father said: "Did you not get up in time to do your hair this morning?" To which, Jane replied airily that it was the latest fashion. But I don't know that he believed her.

'Talking about Father being tough. He certainly was very hardy. I believe he had a cold seawater bath every day. And he never wore an overcoat.'

And indeed, as we can see in the last picture ever taken of him, out on the Maryport foreshore at the age of ninety—he is wearing nothing over his jacket!

'Captain W. A. Nelson', said an obituary in 1929, 'had a worldwide reputation for quick passages. He was almost as well known in Liverpool, San Francisco, Valparaiso and Sydney as in Maryport. One of the most successful masters that ever commanded a sailing ship, he could with an ordinary full-lined ship out-clip the clippers . . . The secret of his success was boldness that never degenerated into recklessness. He drove his ship under press of sail but he was one of the best judges of weather that ever scanned the horizon and if he thought the safety of the ship and the men carried called for it, he did not hesitate to shorten sail.

'Two other factors were that he was a just man and saw that the crew were properly fed, with the result that while he was a strict disciplinarian his discipline was cheerfully accepted . . . He was a thorough sailor. Periodically he examined all rigging and equipment and hence he knew he could depend on it, and his men knowing his capability as a master, knew they could depend on him and had full confidence in his judgment . . . Sail has fought a losing fight with steam, but it would have fared better and lasted longer had all the masters been of the type of this Maryport captain.'

But William Nelson's most fitting epitaph is surely that provided, unwittingly, by his old friend Thomas Ritson, the Maryport shipowner and builder. The master who had succeeded William in one of Ritsons' ships was making slow voyages and Ritson wanted an explanation.

'Light winds, sir,' explained the skipper blandly. And it was light winds here and light winds there, until the forthright Ritson became impatient. 'How is it,' he asked, 'that Captain Nelson was never delayed by light winds?'

'Luck, sir,' shrugged the skipper, fertile in excuses. 'Just good luck.'

'Good luck be damned!' exploded Ritson. 'I call it good seamanship.'

Epilogue

As William Nelson's career came to an end, that of his son James was in full flow. The completion of the *Acamas*'s sixth voyage had seen the end of James's apprenticeship to the Ritsons, and straight away he sat and passed his examinations for second mate. After making a voyage as third mate in steam from Antwerp to ports on the River Plate, he went as second mate in the barque *Inverness*—a vessel whose portrait he painted several times with skill and sensitivity.

After leaving the *Inverness*, James passed his first mate's examination and returned to steam for good. In August, 1910, having obtained his master's certificate, he joined Alfred Holt's famous Blue Funnel Line of Liverpool, with whom he stayed until his retirement in 1953.

Meanwhile, James Nelson's lifelong friend Thomas Brabban Marsham, fellow apprentice aboard the *Acamas*, had also completed his time with Messrs Ritsons. Like James, he recognized the rapid decline of the sailing ship and of the Cumbrian ports, and in 1910, when he secured his master's certificate, he too joined the Blue Funnel Line.

In August, 1914, at the outbreak of war, both men volunteered for the Royal Naval Reserve and were on active service until 1919, after which they returned to Blue Funnel, quickly rising to command in the demanding schedules of the Far East liner trade. Twenty years later came the second World War.

In 1940, as Convoy Commodore in the S.S. *Autolycus*, Captain James Nelson was not long in gaining experience of the problems posed by air attack. In 1942 he took command of the newly-built Blue Funnel fast-supply ship *Priam*. On her maiden voyage, heavily loaded with a cargo of army tanks, aircraft, mines, ammunition and explosives, she encountered exceptionally heavy weather off the West African coast. In a near-sinking condition, down by the head, her forward holds flooded, and with the explosives in her cargo becoming so dangerous that she was forbidden to enter port, she was saved (to quote the citation) 'by magnificent seamanship'.

During the same year, in the Blue Funnel ship *Orestes*, Captain Thomas Brabban Marsham proved that he, too, had acquired his share of his old captain's 'Nelson Touch'. On one occasion, 'this resourceful ship's master' refloated his vessel, unaided, off the South Africa coast after she had grounded while zig-zagging to avoid a U-boat. This feat, accomplished under conditions of great hazard, entailed the laying-out of the main anchor, as a kedge, slung between two ship's life-boats. Later, 'Captain Marsham's brilliant handling of his ship and armaments' enabled him to beat off a Japanese air attack during the 1942 Easter raid on Ceylon. Later still, when attacked by three Japanese submarines, he not only saved the *Orestes* by skilful manoeuvring but hit back at the enemy by dropping depth charges at maximum setting—having purposely allowed one submarine to come close astern.

Depth charges had been fitted to a small number of fast merchant ships, but this engagement seems to have been the only occasion when they were used in action—and with effect!

'When my father was fighting off Japanese aircraft and submarines from the *Orestes*,' writes Thomas Nelson Marsham, 'I was also in eastern waters making my first voyage on her sister ship the *Idomeneus*.

'While the *Orestes* was in Fremantle being repaired after the shellburst and fire damage sustained in the submarine attack, we happened to be passing nearby Rottnest—an island mentioned in my grandfather's logs and memoirs. My father, hearing that the *Idomeneus* was so close, used his influence with the Navy to have us anchor off Fremantle, so that I could dash ashore to see him.

'This was the first and only time we met while I was at sea. The voyage of the *Orestes* proved to be his last. As a result of the stress he had suffered he died soon afterwards, his death being attributed directly to war service.

'The parallels between his career and that of his brother-in-law, my uncle James, are almost uncanny. Both joined Messrs Ritsons in 1902. Both were apprentices under Captain W. A. Nelson. Both got their master's certificates and joined Holt's Blue Funnel Line as third officers in the same year, 1910.* They served together as naval officers during the first World War; were married during the same year, 1915; became Blue Funnel Line captains in 1927 and maintained the closest contact until the second World War, in the course of which both received the O.B.E—won during 1942.

'The exploits from their wartime service quoted above, merely two picked out from many displays of fine seamanship, illustrate the benefit both my uncle and my father derived from their training under my grandfather, whose leadership and perfectionist attitude to ship-handling I heard them praise on many occasions.

*It may seem strange that the holder of a master's certificate would start as a third officer. But the Blue Funnel Line, as befitted that famous company, was very demanding. Only the best men were taken on and a master's certificate was obligatory. Newcomers started as third officers and were promoted on merit. Command of a Blue Funnel liner was one of the highest honours in the Merchant Service of the time.

'It is pleasing to record that the Nelson family maritime tradition has been maintained. My own ambition to make a career as a navigator was not fulfilled due to colour blindness; but I did serve at sea for five years during the war as a radio officer. Since then I have spent much of my spare time sailing in the Solway with friends and members of my family; latterly in the yacht *Rising Star*—namesake of the famous ship commanded by Captain Nelson.

'My experience of the strong tidal streams and shifting sand-banks of the Solway does much to strengthen my admiration of those seamen who regularly sailed their much less handy square-riggers, not only in these waters but to nearly every part of the globe.

'Today as I write, a great-grandson of Captain W. A. Nelson (my son Phillip), is completing his training as a deck officer with Ocean Fleets (the successor to Blue Funnel). And so the Nelson seafaring strain maintains an unbroken line.'

As one might expect, the Nelsons of Maryport succeeded in adapting to the rapidly changing conditions of the age they lived in. It remains to be seen whether Maryport itself can adapt to present-day economics, recapture some of its former glory, and find a new role in the maritime world of tomorrow.

The Final Analysis

Mr Robert Ritson of the Maryport shipbuilding firm, writing to a friend, mentions 'the astonishing consistency of Captain Nelson's sailing'. This consistency is strikingly revealed by the *Summary of Passages*. Among his many voyages, in a series of passages totalling over 100,000 miles, William's best and worst times differ from the average only by about 5%—roughly equivalent to a variation of ten minutes in a three-hour train journey.

In my experience, this consistency of rail service is seldom achieved, even though the train is spared the rigours of a beat to windward round Cape Horn!

Summary of passages made by Captain W. A. Nelson*

Date	Ship	From	To	Av. M/D	Days	Dist. sailed
1887	*Mary Moore*	United Kingdom	W. Coast S. America (shortest) (longest)	140 125	78 88	
1888	*William Ritson*	Garston	Iquique	114	95	10,878
1889	*William Ritson*	Carrizal	Queenstown	131	89	11,632
1889	*Rising Star*	Antwerp	Valparaiso	149	66	9,847
1890	*Rising Star*	Iquique	Falmouth	118	93	10,985
1890	*Rising Star*	Tyne	Valparaiso	102	94	9,613
1891	*Rising Star*	Iquique	Falmouth	109	107	11,683
1891	*Auchencairn*	Cardiff	San Francisco	130	118	15,336
1893	*Auchencairn*	San Francisco	Queenstown	141	111	15,682
1894	*Auchencairn*	Tyne	Port Pirie (Aus:)	155	86	13,297
1894	*Auchencairn*	Newcastle NSW	San Francisco	129	64	8,250

Note: Many of the times claimed for sailing ships' passages as quoted in various newspapers and nautical publications tend to be exaggerated. Sometimes, even, the dates when the passages are said to have been made are incorrect. The passage times listed below are from Captain W. A. Nelson's log-books and have been checked by two ship's masters.

Date	Ship	From	To	Av. M/D	Days	Dist. sailed
1896	*Auchencairn*	Antwerp	Port Pirie (Aus:)	177	74	13,080
1896	*Auchencairn*	Port Pirie (Aus:)	San Francisco	174	61	10,608
1897	*Auchencairn*	San Francisco	Queenstown	134	120	16,039
1897	*Acamas*	Newport	Geraldton (Aus:)	159	78	12,432
1898	*Acamas*	Newcastle NSW	San Francisco	115	72	8,245
1898	*Acamas*	Steveston BC	Liverpool	119	140	16,678
1899	*Acamas*	Liverpool	Calcutta	139	104	14,497
1899	*Acamas*	Calcutta	Hamburg	139	102	14,185
1900	*Acamas*	Hamburg	San Francisco	133	125	16,612
1900	*Acamas*	San Francisco	Falmouth	125	124	15,554
1901	*Acamas*	Barry Dock	Port Germain	154	88	13,575
1901	*Acamas*	Newcastle NSW	Valparaiso	146	45	6,571
1902	*Acamas*	Taltal	Rotterdam	115	100	11,500
1902	*Acamas*	Barry Dock	Algoa Bay	132	61	8,032
1903	*Acamas*	Algoa Bay	Newcastle NSW	133	43	5,707
1903	*Acamas*	Newcastle NSW	San Francisco	122	72	8,797
1903	*Acamas*	San Francisco	Fremantle WA	108	84	3,067
1904	*Acamas*	Fremantle WA	Newcastle NSW	155	16	2,478
1904	*Acamas*	Newcastle NSW	San Francisco	107	75	8,045
1905	*Acamas*	Eureka Cal:	Queenstown	118	136	15,975
1905	*Acamas*	Port Talbot	Pisagua	101	109	11,033
1906	*Acamas*	Antofagasta	Rotterdam	113	99	11,186

('Beat *Dalgonar* by at least a week')

| 1907 | *Ladas* | Liverpool | Callao (Put into Monte Video) |
| 1908 | *Ladas* | Taltal | Antwerp ('Average passage' logged) |

Glossary of Nautical Terms

AB: 'Able-bodied' or first-rate seaman.

Aback: To be 'taken aback': to have the square sails blown backwards against the masts by a sudden and unexpected shift of wind.

Abaft: Behind, or towards the stern of, a vessel. 'Abaft the beam.'

Abeam: At right angles to a vessel, amidships. 'Wind abeam.'

Aft: The after or stern part of a vessel; or behind the vessel itself.

Aloft: Overhead. In the upper rigging or on the yards.

Amidships: The middle part of a vessel.

Astern: Behind a vessel; in her wake. 'To go astern': to go backwards.

Back: To 'back' a sail is to haul it to windward—e.g., when heaving-to. When the wind 'backs' it moves in an anti-clockwise direction. When the wind 'veers' it moves in a clockwise direction.

Baffling: A baffling wind is one that is constantly shifting. Hence 'baffling' boards: baffles used to restrict the shifting of loose cargo such as coal.

Barque: A vessel having three or more masts, with fore-and-aft rig on the after mast. A three-masted barque would have square rig on fore and main masts; fore-and-aft rig on the mizzen.

Barquentine: A three-masted vessel, square-rigged on the foremast, fore-and-aft rigged on main and mizzen masts.

Beam: The width of a vessel at her widest part. 'On the beam', at right angles to the vessel amidships. A ship is on her 'beam ends' when thrown over on her side—the result, perhaps, of heavy seas, strong winds, a shifting cargo.

Beating: Sailing on a course dead to windward. 'Tacking' close-hauled towards the wind in a series of zig-zags.

Before the mast: To serve before the mast: to ship as a deck hand as opposed to an officer. An officer's living quarters were in the after part of the ship. The seamen's usually in the forward part—often in the forecastle (or fo'c'stle) in front of (before) the foremast.

Belaying pin: A pin of wood or metal round which a rope, usually a halyard, is made fast (belayed).

Bend: To fasten. To 'bend' one rope to another: a sail to a spar; a cable to an anchor. When sails are laced in position on their spars, they are 'bent'.

Berth: The place in which a vessel is moored. On board ship, a berth is a cabin, a bed or bunk, or space for swinging a hammock.

Bight: A loop in a rope. An inlet or bay along a coastline.

Binnacle: Non-magnetic housing of a vessel's compass, which also contains the means of illumination as well as the compensating magnets that correct compass deviation.

Bitts: Small posts fixed through the deck, usually at the foot of the bowsprit, serving as cleats.

Blue Peter: A blue flag with white square in centre, flown to signal a vessel's departure.

Blue-nose: Nova Scotian ship or sailor.

Board: A tack or leg when beating to windward. To make a long 'board': to travel a long distance on the same tack. A mast 'gone by the board' is one that has broken off close to the deck.

Boarding-house runner: Crimp's assistant.

Bob-stay: A stay of wire or chain from the nose of the bowsprit to the vessel's stempost.

Bonnet: Additional canvas laced to the foot of a standing sail to increase its area. Used in light winds.

Boom: A spar extending the *head* of a stun'sail (studding sail), hence stun'sail boom. But also, the spar that extends the *foot* of a fore-and-aft sail such as the spanker. Hence spanker-boom. A jib-boom, however, is an extension to the bowsprit.

Bo'sun (boatswain): The crew's foreman, whose duties include care of sails and rigging.

Bo'sun's chair: A seat, rather like the seat of a swing, which can be hauled aloft by a rope from the masthead.

Bower anchor: One of a vessel's two big anchors carried at the bows.

Bows: The stem or forward part of a vessel.

Bowsprit: The spar projecting forward from a vessel's stem, which (sometimes with a jib-boom) supports the headsails or 'jibs'.

Braces: Ropes that control the trimming of squaresail yards.

Broadside: Sideways. As in broadside (or sideways) launching.

Brig: A two-masted vessel, square-rigged on both masts, but also having a gaff-mainsail.

Brigantine: A two-masted vessel, square-rigged on foremast, fore-and-aft rigged on mainmast.

Bulkheads: Partitions helping to form cabins, or to divide a hold into watertight compartments.

Bulwarks: The sides of a vessel above deck level.

Buntlines: Lines fastened to the footrope of a squaresail that pass round the sail's forward side and gather it up to its yard when being furled.

Burton: A tackle consisting of several pulleys used to set-up or tighten rigging, or to shift heavy weights.

By the wind (full and by): Sailing with the wind forward of the beam. Close-hauled.

Cable: Any heavy rope or chain for towing or other purposes. The rope or chain holding a vessel's anchor. Cable's length: approximately 200 yards. 'To slip the cable': to let go the anchor chain or rope in emergency.

Carry-on: To keep as much sail set as possible for as long as possible.

Caulking: Filling the seams between a vessel's planks with oakum, then paying them with hot pitch.

Chops of the Channel: The western entrance.

Clipper: Any merchant vessel of any size or rig designed primarily for speed.

Cleat: A small wedge of wood or iron, usually with two arms, bolted to mast, coaming, or spar for fastening a rope.

Clews: The lower corners of a squaresail. To 'clew-up': to gather up the corners of the sail by its 'clew-lines' or 'garnets'.

Close-hauled: Sailing as near to the wind as possible.

Coaming: A raised edge round a hatchway, or round the cockpit of a small sailing boat.

Come-to: Luff up, head into wind. Bring the vessel's bows towards the wind.

Composite: A system of ship-building using iron frames with wooden planking.

Counter: The part of a vessel that extends aft beyond her sternpost.

Course: The lowest (and largest) squaresail on a mast.

Coppers: 'Hot coppers': throat parched through excessive drinking.

Crank: Tender; lacking in stiffness. A vessel that is crank (for whatever reason; perhaps cargo stowage) has too high a centre of gravity and cannot, therefore, 'carry-on' owing to the danger of overturning.

Crimps: Longshore sharks who boarded sailors, found them ships—and robbed them.

Crossjack: The lowest yard on the mizzenmast of a full-rigged ship.

Davits: The small curved cranes on a vessel's sides for hoisting and lowering the lifeboats.

Dead horse: Labour paid for in advance. 'To work off a dead horse.'

Dodger: A wind-screen, usually of canvas.

Dog-watches: Two short watches (or spells on deck) of two hours each, from 4 to 6 p.m. and from 6 to 8 p.m., used to shift the watches each night so that the same watch is not on deck at the same hours. Ordinary watches being of four hours.

Donkey's breakfast: Straw mattress.

Donkey engine: A small engine for working derricks, hauling cables, etc.

Draught (draft): The maximum depth of a vessel underwater, varying with the state of her loading.

Driver (or spanker): The gaff-sail on the mizzenmast of a full-rigged ship.

Easting: 'Running the easting down': sailing in an easterly direction in high southern latitudes where fair winds prevail.

Embayed: Trapped within an inlet into which the wind is blowing; so that, in order to escape, the vessel must beat to windward.

Fairlead: Any ring, channel, bolt or eye on a vessel's deck that guides a rope in a required direction.

Fall (of a rope): The part of a rope that is hauled upon.

Fathom: A depth of water: six feet.

Fender: A cushion, usually of rope, inserted between two vessels lying side by side in harbour; or between a vessel and the harbour wall.

Flotsam: Anything found floating in the sea.

Forecastle (or fo'c'sle, pronounced 'fokes'l') The forward deck, often raised above the main deck. The space beneath was usually the crew's quarters.

Footrope: The rope beneath a yard on which the crew stand when reefing or furling a sail. A sail's 'footrope' is the boltrope along its foot, or bottom edge.

Foremast: The mast nearest the bows of a vessel—except in the case of small vessels such as ketches and yawls, when the forward mast becomes the mainmast; the other mast, the mizzen.

Foresail: In square-riggers, the foresail is the fore 'course', the largest and lowest of the sails set on the foremast. In vessels of fore-and-aft rig, it is either:
  (a) In schooners, the gaff-sail on the foremast, or
  (b) In cutters, ketches and yawls, the triangular sail extending from the lower mast-head to the stem-head.

Fore-and-aft: Fore-and-aft sails are those set along the direction of a line drawn from stem to stern: jibs, staysails, gaff-sails and gaff-topsails.

Freeboard: That part of a vessel's side which is free of the water. The distance from the load water-line to the deck at the shortest point.

Fothering: A method of stopping a leak in hull or hatch. A sail is covered thickly with oakum or rope-yarn.

This 'packing' is sucked into the leak, over which the sail is drawn tight and fastened.

Furling: Stowing a sail and tying it to its boom or yard. 'Furling lines', also called 'gaskets' are short ropes used for securing the sail.

Gaff: The spar that extends the top edge or 'head' of a fore-and-aft sail such as the spanker of a ship, or the mainsail and foresail of a schooner.

Gaskets: The ropes securing a sail when furled. Also called 'ties' and 'furling-lines'.

G.M.T. Greenwich Mean Time.

Goose-wing: A squaresail 'goosewinged' is when the bunt (the middle part) is hauled up to the yard while the clews (the lower corners) hang. Sometimes used for reducing sail, or when scudding (running before the wind). In fore-and-aft rig, to sail goose-winged is to sail straight before the wind with sails boomed out on both sides.

Half-deck: In old ships of war the half-deck extended from the mainmast to the quarter-deck. In windjammers it was the name commonly given to the apprentices' living quarters.

Hard-tack: Ship's biscuit.

Halyard: A rope by which a sail or spar is hoisted.

Hawse-pipes: Short metal tubes lining the holes in a vessel's bows through which the hawser or cable runs.

Head A vessel is down by the head (or stem) when out of trim due to her bows being too low in the water.

Headsails: All fore-and-aft sails set ahead of the foremast.

Heave-to: To bring a vessel head to wind with some of her sails 'backed' or sheeted to windward. A vessel thus hove-to makes very little forward progress.

Hoist: To haul up. Also, a number of flags hoisted together as a signal: a 'signal hoist'.

Holystone: A soft sandstone used for scouring a vessel's deck planks.

House: To lower or 'strike' any of the upper masts. A topmast lowered and fastened to the lower mast is said to be 'housed'.

Jettison: To cast goods overboard.

Jetsam: The meaning of 'jetsam' is rather vague. The common definition (distinguishing it from flotsam) is: anything cast overboard that sinks and is later washed ashore.

Jib: The foremost of the triangular headsails. There may be several jibs set ahead of the forestaysail: inner-jib, outer-jib and flying-jib.

Jib-boom: An extension to the bowsprit that supports the flying-jib.

Jigger: The fourth mast (after fore, main and mizzen) in a four-masted vessel.

Jury-rig: A temporary or substitute rig employed after a vessel has lost masts or spars in some emergency.

Kedge: An anchor, smaller than the main anchors, used for 'kedging-off' or 'kedge-hauling'.

Kedging-off: Running out a kedge on a long warp by ship's boat to haul a grounded vessel into deeper water.

Kedge-hauling: Working a vessel against tide, or in narrow waters, by means of kedges.

Ketch: A two-masted (main and mizzen) fore-and-aft rigged vessel, the mizzen mast being shorter than the mainmast and stepped forward of the rudder post.

Knot: A nautical mile per hour. (It is not a measurement of distance. 'Ten knots per hour' is a solecism. The vessel would be travelling at ten knots.)

Lanyards: Short pieces of rope having various uses at sea—generally the tightening-down of a stay through deadeyes or thimbles.

Lee, leeward: The side away from the wind. The side on which the wind is blowing is the 'windward' or 'weather' side. One speaks of an object being 'to windward' or 'to leeward'. The lee of a rock: the sheltered side, away from the wind.

Leech: The aftermost or outside margin of a sail.

Lighter: A strongly-built, flat-bottomed barge, usually propelled by long sweeps, or oars, used for transporting goods to or from a vessel.

Limbers: Apertures in a vessel's bulwarks or coamings.

Limejuicer: A British windjammer of the late 19th-century. (See also, p. 35)

List: An inclination. To list: to lean over. Thus, a vessel is said to be listing to starboard, or port.

Log: The ship's log was the instrument used for measuring the vessel's speed. 'Log' is often used to mean log-book.

Log-book: A journal containing a vessel's daily position and events, kept by the master.

Mainmast: The principal mast. (Middle mast in a full-rigged ship or three-masted barque; front mast in ketch or yawl.)

Mainsail: The principal sail on the mainmast (the 'main 'course' on a square-rigged vessel).

Making sail: Setting sail.

Marks (down to): 'Down to her marks': a vessel fully cargoed, down to the loading marks on the vessel's sides.

Marling: To marl: to wind any small line

round a rope so that every turn is secured by a knot.

Marling spike: A smooth, round, pointed instrument used for opening the strands of rope or wire when splicing, or marling.

Messenger: The endless chain which, in some vessels, was coupled to the forward winch to provide the motive power for the windlass. A rope which, being attached to a heavy cable, is hauled in by a capstan, the cable itself being too large to grip the barrel. The messenger is often attached to the cable by smaller ropes called 'nippers', and is then said to be 'nipped on'.

Mizzenmast: The aftermost mast in yawls, ketches, three-masted barques and full-rigged ships. In a five-masted vessel the mizzenmast is astern of the foremast and mainmast but forward of the jigger and spanker.

Moonraker: Sometimes called 'moonsail'. A squaresail set above the skysail, for use in very light airs.

Nautical mile: One sixtieth of a degree of latitude: 6,046 feet.

Neap tides: Slack tides, with small rise and fall.

Ordinary seaman: A deck-hand, able to make himself useful even to working aloft, but not a first-rate sailor; the latter being termed an able-bodied seaman, or A.B.

Parrel: A band of rope; a chain, or iron collar, by which the middle of a yard is fastened to the mast.

Pay-off: To sheer away from the wind. Square away.

Peak: The upper end of a gaff. Also, the uppermost corner of a sail carried by a gaff.

Poop: The after part of a vessel. A vessel is said to be 'pooped' when a sea comes aboard and over the stern.

Port: 'Port' side: the left-hand side of a vessel, looking towards the bows.

Quarter: A vessel's quarters are those portions of the sides about halfway between beam and stern. They correspond with the vessel's 'bows', which lie forward of the beam.

Quarterdeck: That portion of the deck covering the 'quarters'.

Quarterly wind: A wind blowing on the vessel's quarter: from about 45° abaft the beam.

Ratlines: Small lines crossing the shrouds of a vessel to form the steps of a ladder by which the crew can climb aloft.

Reefing: Reducing the area of a sail spread to the wind.

Ring-bolt: A bolt with a ring at its head, usually passed through one of the vessel's strong timbers, for the attachment of a tackle.

Ringtail: A kind of stun'sail; a narrow additional strip of canvas set beyond the leech of a gaff-mainsail or a spanker.

Rovings: Rope bands. Ravellings of canvas or bunting.

Royal: The small mast above (and usually in one piece with) the topgallant mast. It takes its name from the mast on which it is fixed: fore-royal; main-royal etc. It is the highest mast in a vessel and carries the royal sail and skysail.

Rudder: The hinged flap (hung upon the stern post) with which a vessel is steered.

Rudder trunk: The casing fitted round the hole through which the rudder stock passes.

Run: Sail before the wind.

Run of a ship: The backward sweep of the underpart of a vessel's hull.

Scrimshaw work: Carvings and fancy ropework fashioned by sailors during their watch below.

Scudding: Running before the wind with little or no canvas set. (See 'goosewing').

Scuttle: To sink a vessel on purpose. Also, an opening in a vessel's sides or deck; e.g. a hatchway.

Sennet: A cord braided out of yarns.

Sheer: 'Taking a sheer': bearing away from. 'Breaking her sheer': the sudden broadside movement of a vessel, either anchored or in tow, due to wind or current; or, perhaps, when in tow, due to faulty steering.

Sheet: Rope attached to the clew of a sail used for trimming the sail according to the set of the wind.

Sheet anchor: A large anchor, formerly the largest of a vessel's anchor, supposed to be used only in emergency.

Shellback: A veteran sailor.

Shifting boards: Partitions placed inside a vessel's hold to help prevent the cargo from moving.

Ship: A 'full-rigged ship': a three-masted vessel, square-rigged on all masts, but also carrying a gaff-sail (spanker or driver) on the mizzenmast.

Shrouds: Wire ropes, set-up by deadeyes or rigging-screws, which provide sideways (athwartships) staying of a mast. (As distinct from 'stays', which provide fore-and-aft support.)

Skids: Raised planks supporting a vessel's lifeboats.

Skysail: The highest sail ordinarily set on a square-rigger. (Sails sometimes set on clipper ships above the skysail in very light airs, were the 'moonraker' and 'jumper'.)

Slip: To 'slip' the anchor: to abandon anchor and cable in an emergency.

Slopchest: The store of bedding, ready-made clothes etc., kept by a ship's master for sale to the crew.

Smack: A small fully-decked merchant or fishing vessel, usually cutter, yawl, or ketch rigged.

Snugging-down: The practice followed by timid masters of reducing sail at sunset to make night sailing less hazardous.

Soul-and-body lashings: Lashings of twine worn around wrists, waist and knees above oilskins to prevent water entering; also, to reduce the chance of being blown off-balance while working aloft in a high wind.

South cone: Storm signal. A black cone hoisted point downwards on a harbour signal-mast indicates gale imminent from the southerly side of the east-west line. A black cone set point upwards signals that a gale is expected from the northerly side.

Sou'wester: An oilskin hat.

Spanker: The gaff-sail on the mizzen mast of a full-rigged ship; also called the 'driver'. The spanker-mast is the fifth on a five-masted vessel counting from the bows: Fore, main, mizzen, jigger, spanker.

Spring tide: The tides at their highest flood and lowest ebb—at the times of full and new moon.

Standard (azimuth) compass: A vessel's master compass, used for taking bearings.

Square away: To ease a vessel off; to bear away from the wind.

Starboard: The right-hand side of a vessel when looking towards the bows. (Opposite to the left-hand or 'port' side.)

Stays: Wire ropes used for the fore-and-aft support of masts, or for the bowsprit (see 'Bob-stay').

Staysails: Apart from the fore topmast staysail, which is a headsail, staysails are set on the stays between the masts: main topmast staysail, main topgallant staysail, main royal staysail, mizzen topmast staysail, mizzen topgallant staysail, mizzen royal staysail, etc.

St Elmo's fire or Corposant: The balls of light sometimes seen on a vessel's masts or yardarms during an electrical storm.

Stern: The after part of a vessel.

Stern-board: The distance a vessel travels stern-first when her sails are aback, either in emergency or when her sails have purposely been trimmed in that fashion; e.g., to refloat the vessel after she has run aground.

Stringers: Strengthening timbers running along the inside of a hull at various distances up the sides.

Stun'sails (studdingsails): Narrow supplementary sails run out on small booms beyond the leeches of the principal square sails.

Tack: To beat to windward. The 'tack' of a sail is the forward lower corner.

Thwart: A seat extending from side to side across a ship's boat.

Thwartships (a'thwartships): From side to side; running *across* the vessel.

Tiller: The handle of a rudder-head with which the rudder can be moved.

Topgallant: The mast above the topmast holding upper and lower topgallantsails.

Topmast: The mast holding the upper and lower topsails.

Topsails: In more recent times, the huge square topsail of the early 19th-century ship—having been found (like the single topgallantsail) to hold too much wind for a comparatively small crew to handle and reef—was divided into two parts called the upper and lower topsails. (The single topgallantsail, too, was divided: into upper and lower topgallants.)

Topsail schooner: A fore-and-aft rigged vessel of two or more masts having two square topsails, or a single square topsail on the foremast.

Topsides: The sides of a vessel between waterline and bulwarks.

Took steam: Engaged a tug, to be towed into or out of port.

Took the ground: Ran aground.

Tommed down: Securely fastened with battens.

Trim: A vessel's trim: her position in the water in relation to the horizontal. If level, she is 'in trim'. If down by the head or stern she is 'out of trim'.

Transoms: Beams bolted across the sternpost to receive the after ends of the decks.

Tuck: To 'take a tuck': to reef a sail. Also, that part of a vessel's stern immediately under her counter terminating under the 'tuck-rail'.

Unbend: To take off: e.g., to unlace a sail from its spar.

Veer: A wind 'veers' when it changes in a clockwise direction: i.e., from north towards east, etc. ('A wind 'backs' when its direction of change is anti-clockwise.)

Waist: The lowest part of the maindeck.

Watches: The division of the crew as equally as possible into two groups called the Port Watch and the Starboard Watch. The watches took it turn and turn about to be on deck in spells of four hours. (But see also, 'Dog-watches'.)

Wear: To 'wear' ship is to put her on the other tack by paying-off and bringing her round stern to wind. The opposite of 'tacking': bringing a ship round head to wind.

Warp: A rope or hawser for securing a vessel to quay or mooring buoy.

Warping: Moving a vessel under the power of her capstan by hauling her up to an anchor laid down ahead, or to a mooring buoy or quay.

Warp and weft: In sailmaking, the warp is the lengthwise measurement of sailcloth, the width being the weft.

Wells: The deepest parts of a vessel in which water accumulates, and from which it is pumped.

Windlass: The wheel and axle, turned with either handspikes or crank, by which the chain cable of a vessel (or any other weight) may be hauled in.

Windjammer: The term (originally derisive) for a latter-day square-rigger.

Windward: Towards the wind. The 'windward' side: the side from which the wind is blowing.

Yard: A spar suspended from the mast and spreading the head of a square-sail.

Yawl: A vessel with two masts, main and mizzen, the mizzen being small and stepped aft of the rudder-post.